I Found Strength In My Struggles

A Purpose to Finish What I Started

TRESSA DEVONNE

© 2017 Tressa Devonne

All rights reserved. This book or parts thereof may not be reproduced in any form, stored in any retrieval system, or transmitted in any form by any means—electronic, mechanical, photocopy, recording, or otherwise—without prior written permission of the publisher, except as provided by United States of America copyright law. For permission requests, contact publisher at info@eventfulconcepts.com

ISBN-13: 978-1546989561

ISBN-10: 1546989560

Acknowledgements

I would like to first thank God for creating me as his creation to execute creativity through my writing, voice and vision. I thank him in advance for the opportunities that open up as a result from this book. The best is yet to come. I want to definitely thank my parents for coming together to bring me in this world as your daughter. God definitely had a plan. I know I am not perfect and I can be distant at times but I love you both to the moon and back. I am so grateful for your support. Special love and thanks to my best friend Jereatha who pushed me even when I didn't want to push myself. Her words of wisdom and continuous prayer kept me motivated to finish what I started. Love you girl! He definitely put you in my life for a reason. Thank you Dexter who encourage me to recognize the strengths within myself. You told me that is was time to operate in my gifts and I thank you for loving me. Thank you Juvy -my mentor for career development into the next level. Your confidence in owning who you are represents commitment to excellence which keeps me inspired. Thank you to My Sisters Keeper leaders and board members who gives me the ability to execute my ideas and creativity while glorifying God. Our sisterhood to collaborate in ministry while empowering other women is priceless. I want to acknowledge family, friends, associates, coworkers, or anyone who I have connected with along the way in this journey.

Dedication

I dedicate this book to my grandmother June Woods who is now in heaven smiling down as my angel. If she was still here she would be so proud of me. Her favorite song was *"Just Another Day That the Lord has Kept Me"* which will always remain in my soul. That song allowed me to fully understand how thankful and grateful I am. Despite the storm, I am still standing. Miss you Granny!

Rest in Peace–February 27, 2015

TABLE OF CONTENTS

Introduction vi
Chapter 1: Finding Purpose 1
Chapter 2: Why not you?...5
Chapter 3: Painkillers And Living In Between 17
Chapter 4: Breaking Free From Childhood Pain 27
Chapter 5: Opportunity Comes With Opposition 32
Chapter 6: Only God Can Judge 40
Chapter 7: Convicted To Grow 44
Chapter 8: Wrestling With Trust...50
Chapter 9: What if 57
Chapter 10: Forgiveness Is Release 60
Chapter 11: It Doesn't Have To Be Your Destiny 67
Chapter 12: Never Settle For The Bare Minimum 74
Chapter 13: Health Matters...82
Chapter 14: Love And Our Timeline 87
Chapter 15: Make Time For Yourself 95
Chapter 16: The Value Of A Dollar..101
Chapter 17: Timing Is Everything 104
Chapter 18: Starting Something New 108
Chapter 19: Anxiety Takeover 112
Chapter 20: Stay Focused 118
Chapter 21: Breaking The Curse 122
Chapter 22: Learned Lessons..127
Chapter 23: Success Despite Obstacles 133
Chapter 24: Live Life Like It Is Golden...................................140
Chapter 25: Taking Time...145
Chapter 26: I Want My Family Back 150
Afterword: The Next Chapter 157

INTRODUCTION

What is my purpose?

So many of us don't know what our purpose is. That is indeed the million dollar question asked by so many who are passionate about finding it. We move through large portions of our lives distraught and lost. There are many folks in this world, from all walks of life, who are still searching for a purpose. No matter what your cultural background, your age, your gender, or your religion, we all share a common goal: to seek the opportunity to live by our purpose with passion and prosper the reward.

Like many of you, I don't want to leave this life not knowing what my purpose is.

So, how do you know?

It took me writing this book, soul searching, and continuous prayer to discover my gifts and my strengths through my struggles while overcoming tribulations in my life. In a way, this book was my therapy and a major portion of my journey in finding and finally accepting the purpose that God had designed for me. This book also serves as my motivation to keep living life and utilizing the gifts I have been blessed with. Believe me when I tell you there were times when I just wanted to throw in the towel and give up on life because I felt like my journey was over. There was a higher purpose that got my attention and said "You have a purpose to finish what you started!" "Don't be selfish, because it's not about you!"

Like many of you, I was sick and tired of being sick and tired. It is ironic that we become sick and tired by trying with eagerness to build a safe, comfortable life for ourselves and our family; to accomplish goals but have no end results. Our struggle to reach satisfaction contributes to making us sick and tired literally. Fear, along with doubt and anxiety, is found and hidden in that complacent comfort zone of our lives.

We come out of high school. The next step for most of us is either straight to college or diving directly into the job market. The traditional goal in the American dream is marriage, kids, and a normal life with a house surrounded by a white picket fence and sometimes a dog or cat to complete the family. But for the new normal, some of us tend to focus in depth on our individual goals or desires that diverges from the traditional path. It is clear that times have changed!

Some of us struggle under financial burdens and use those as excuses to hold ourselves back from reaching for anything greater than we can imagine or hope for. Dreams are just dreams; they could never come true in the average person's mind. We settle for our current way of life rather than stepping out in faith to achieve the goals that are exceedingly and abundantly available beyond our dreams.

In our minds, dreams are only a happy distraction – not a true purpose in life. Our lives are perfectly built to ignore our purposes for years or even a lifetime. No one dies regretting having found their purpose in life, regardless of their struggle, but how many people leave this life never finding a purpose? I want my obituary to be a promotional flyer that demonstrates my life achievements and the struggles that I overcame as a way to inspire others to continue to press forward and go after their dreams. I always say I want to finish what I started. I don't want to leave any unfinished business or task incomplete because of procrastination or lack of commitment on my part.

I am Tressa and this is my story. I share it now on these pages because I know there are women that need to hear these tough truths. There are people that need to be lifted up by someone who has been where they are and has learned from the same things they are going through. Maybe you need to know that there is a way out and a way up from some very low points in life. I've been on this rollercoaster of highs and lows. I know what a painful ride it can be.

People naturally face obstacles and roadblocks because living life without regrets is itself a struggle. But, we put up with struggle without ever finding out what it all meant for our purpose. You must believe you have the power within yourself to succeed.

Not everyone is spiritually led, but for me, I prayed and I kept praying over and over and over again. I used the PUSH factor, which is to *Pray Until Something Happens*. It wasn't an overnight breakthrough. It took years of continuous falling and getting back up until I finally put forth the effort to search for my purpose and own the struggles I had that stopped me from finding it. Even at my worst, which I will show you in a very real way in the chapters of this book, I still prayed. I prayed even when I wasn't really listening for an answer. I prayed when I was as low as any of you may be feeling at the moment or have felt at one point in time. This is not a book about how I have it all together and all figured out, because I'm not perfect. In fact, I am still learning who I am as a woman. Specifically, I am still learning who I am as a unique and creative individual. I started writing this book in 2014 and it took a year to finish it. Three years later, I am still tweaking and adding to the book and finally came to grips with the fact that I need to complete it. Anything else that I leave out or need to add can be put in my next book, titled *"Don't Expect Results if There is No Change"*. Crazy as it may sound, why am I thinking about the second book when I am still trying to publish this book? My mind is like a merry go round- there are always ideas and visions that revolve around my head, which amazes me at times. That's why I need to finish what I started - which starts by publishing this book so you have the chance to read the journey of me finding strengths in my struggles. There are a lot of personal, dark moments of my life in these chapters. It scares me, but I believe it will help those still searching for a little guidance to keep pressing on. We are all human beings, and we all have sin and fall short at some point in our lives. As I write this book, I am still picking myself up, but it is not too late for you to join me in this journey too. Writing this book is a transformation for me, and I want reading it to be a transformation for you. You have to go through the process in order to obtain success.

What I can say is that I am truly blessed and grateful. My spiritual connection with God is at a different level right now. In my past prayers, I would often question God about why I was in certain situations or why things would happen to me. I questioned him so many times that eventually my questions turned into prayers of thanks and gratefulness. I grew in my faith and He became my way out of nowhere. He showed me doors of opportunity that I could not see before. Now I am able to say thank you for never leaving me nor forsaking me. I am still learning how to exercise my faith through continuous prayer and by surrounding myself with positivity.

Whether you are spiritual or not, I believe my story holds something for you. We all fall, but we can all get back up through perseverance and tenacity. You may be living a life that is a journey of two steps forward and getting knocked ten steps back. The key is to never give up – continue the fight.

Your purpose is still there to be found and these pages are about finding it.

CHAPTER 1: FINDING PURPOSE

In my early twenties, I wanted to be an actress and then a writer but God spoke and said, *"Not this time"*. I tried to start a women's group about ten years ago called NDpendent Lady with the ND meaning "Naturally Dynamic". It was meant to empower, engage, and elevate women while building a platform of networking for diverse women to enhance their career, finances, well-being, and personal growth. After a little success, I ran into a roadblock, and I shut it down. God spoke to me and said, *"You are not ready"*, followed by *in due time"*. I understand now why patience is the key while following the process to get to the promise. I started Eventful Concepts to coordinate corporate events and networking mixers. I did a few gigs, but hit some snags and let that go too. God clearly spoke and said, *"Revaluate yourself."* Other ventures went the same way for me as well.

Why did these things fail for me? I would question God at times asking him why was I given all these creative and sometimes crazy ideas and they never came to fruition. You see there are ordinary people and there are extraordinary people that think outside the box. It wasn't a mistake that these thoughts, business ventures, or career moves failed; it was that I wasn't fully equipped to execute success. Lack of training, not being mentored by someone who had done it before, or just not being in the right mindset caused me to be less eager to finish what I started.

What I've come to realize is that the minute that something came along as a roadblock, I quit. I didn't like the challenges or steps to reaching the accomplishment. I wanted every step to be fast and easy, without any hindrance stopping me along the way. Instead of taking the time to find a solution, I was too quick to give up and my ventures failed. A best friend of mine once said to me you have to go through the process in order to get to the promise.

I should have been looking at those roadblocks as blowouts instead. You see, if my tire blew out on my car on the way to work, I wouldn't just step out of the car and walk home never to return again. Instead, I would change the tire myself or call roadside assistance to help. I would make sure I solved the problem and found my way to work somehow. In retrospect, we need to live through blowouts by finding solutions, not treating roadblocks as ended journeys.

Then, there are the people in your ear saying, "Girl, that won't work. That won't make you any money. That idea is stupid." Well let me tell you - there is no stupid idea. The definition of an idea is a thought or collection of thoughts that generate in the mind. I realize my ideas and adventures to start something didn't manifest like I wanted them to, but that isn't to say the ideas were stupid. It just wasn't my season to execute. After years and years of trying new things, I understand the importance of preplanning and research before implementing your idea. Who would've thought Eventful Concepts would be revamped into something totally different than what I had originally envisioned? Who would've thought NDpendent Lady would come back to me in a vision 10 years later, followed by a plan to execute? These stories are key to concepts in later chapters.

Maybe it is time for a few stupid ideas, but in hindsight, there is no stupid idea. Just look around you right now. Every invention you see was someone's stupid idea that the dream killers said would never work or that they never had the vision to imagine. The truth is that ideas are useless to those who don't believe in letting your vision become a reality. To people with purpose, stupid ideas are actually dreams worthy of risk.

Whether your dream is to own your own business or to achieve something creative, sometimes you can't tell everybody until your vision is executed. Be selective with whom you share your aspirations because there are plenty of dream killers out there and that negativity will water down your dreams in a hurry. If you are nodding along right now, you have felt that same negativity and buckled under it.

There are times we must step out of that comfort zone and whatever version of normal we have built up for ourselves. We have to step out in faith. There may be poisonous relationships, a toxic work environment, or areas where bad choices are made easy; these situations call us to step out in faith. We need to step out to find the people and opportunities that will aid us in being better and achieving our purpose.

Writing this book is an anxious experience for me. I spoke with someone I trusted about it, and her response was encouragement to me. But for herself, she said, "What am I going to do at my age?"

She is about 15 years older than me and I respectfully believe she is selling herself short. The answer to that question is that she can do anything she puts her mind to. I took her encouragement to me and her discouragement for herself as a warning to not live my life in a way that I reach the "what am I going to do at my age" phase - ever.

So how do you know?

It is difficult. Some people have their future figured out at a younger age. The majority of people are still searching. Many more are putting their purpose on the back burner to take care of other things – everyday life gets in their way.

But this is my time now and it can be yours too. Now is my time. Now is your time. Now is the time to make an impact and build a life of purpose.

If you were to take a piece of paper and make two columns, you could get started. In the first column you would make a list of all your God –given talents. In the second column, identify your passions. If you can sing, but it isn't your passion, maybe that tells us something important about why we quit so easily. What keeps you going? Compare the two columns. Pray and meditate on what you see. Then, use the confirmation and revelations to act.

This is the beginning of finding purpose. God does not give you talents that are out of line with your purpose. At the very least, these serve as clues to help you define what you are really meant to do with your life.

As I will discuss in this book, God would reveal to me that the connecting factor of my talents, passion, and purpose. I am meant to use all this and the struggles I experienced to help others. In addition, these upcoming chapters will deal with relationships, self-medicating, gambling, abuse, weight gain, depression, anxiety, low self-esteem, loneliness, communication, fear, faith, and more.

My struggles are real and I'm going to share them in a blunt, raw way. Many of you are going through similar things I experienced and you can find your purpose too. Join me and we can continue this journey together.

CHAPTER 2: WHY NOT YOU?

This was not the first time I found myself broken and feeling less worthy. It was not the first time I asked God a question and had to wait on an answer. This answer was not the first time I had to make a choice in life based on faith. These words and this book come from a leap of faith and an answer I received just four weeks before these words were written.

It wasn't the first time I found myself on my knees asking questions of God and it probably wouldn't be the last time either. I said, "Lord, I need your help. Please, Lord, please, help me. I cry out to you as I am ready to throw in the towel and give up. Enough is enough. Why me?"

Silence. Silence is a painful answer. Sometimes the silence is part of the answer, but sometimes silence is what we hear because we aren't listening or we are ignoring the answer - and that sounds an awful lot like silence.

As I wait for God to respond back to me, hours went by and there was nothing. The next day I asked again, "Lord, did you not hear my prayer? I need your help. Give me the strength for me to continue the journey. Why me?"

I heard that same suspicious silence again. Hours passed by and nothing.

On the third day, I asked again, "Lord, did you not hear my prayer? I need your help. I am ready to fulfill my purpose, but I have no direction on where I'm supposed to go or what I am supposed to do. Why me?"

I am not the kind of person who hears voices. I wanted to hear God's voice as clear as a bell many times in my life. I wanted clear answers spoken to me, out loud, in an unmistakable voice. I wanted to hear God's voice the way I couldn't stop hearing the voices around me that pulled me down, discouraged me, and made me feel like less than I could be. I wanted to hear a voice telling me the opposite of all those negative voices I've heard throughout my life.

Then, there was a chill in the room and goose bumps magically appeared on both of my arms. That sounds so small and unimportant, but it was a very real sensation. A cold draft like a wind blowing over me, and through me, came in that moment.

Then, He finally answered back. This was not the first time He had spoken, but I wasn't always listening. Sometimes I was ignoring Him, and that sounds a lot like silence. I believe God inhabits people with truth, with messages for us. I know He tried with me many times before this moment, but I so often heard the negative voices in my life – voices of people I let into my life that were no good for me, and negative words I spoke to myself in my own head - words that dragged me down.

On this day, I did not hear a voice out loud, but I heard an answer that cut through to my soul. Where my ears refused to listen, my heart heard the answer clearly that day, the third day I asked my question.

I cried and vigorously spoke out loud, "Why me Lord?"

And He said, "Why *not* you?" Silence came over me and to be sure, I repeated my plea again, "Why me?" In the back of my mind I was hoping to hear something different, or at least making myself believe my mind was playing tricks on me. Nope, it wasn't. The silence stretched out as I patiently waited and as plain as day he answered, "Why not you, Tressa? You have a purpose and I know you are aware of that, but I need you to acknowledge and trust me to guide you in the right direction. Again, I can guide you, but it is up to you to make a choice and believe that you can do all things through me who has strengthened you. The question is: Are you ready for the journey I have for you according to my plan? I don't need to give you any more strength. You have it already. Without struggle, you wouldn't have developed strength."

In that moment, I realized something I had been told more than once. I realized my purpose was my voice, my experiences, my obstacles, and my outcomes. That was a strange realization for me because I heard the country girl in my voice; I had followed many passions before that I thought were my purpose. Now my calling was to use my voice to inspire, encourage and empower others. I am supposed to be the voice for others inhabited with truth, bringing the messages that others in the midst of struggles, especially women like me, can hear. They need to know that there is still hope to be found.

There was a long, hard journey that led to this particular set of questions and answers. There were some very low points that lead me to that day of asking, "Why me?

There was a day, a Friday night in January of 2001, which cannot be ignored in my journey. It was only recently that it occurred to me that this was the day I can point to as the real beginning of my struggles with lack of trust, lack of commitment, low self-esteem, excessive alcohol drinking, self -medication, anxiety, depression, weight gain, and the financial woes of my life. That is not an excuse or a way of ignoring all the other choices I made in my life before and after that day, but it is the reality of this particular day.

Prior to 2001, I was in a toxic relationship for several years and was afraid to leave. I was in denial that this was an abusive situation whether it was emotionally or physically. The extent of the abuse and my aunt's tragic passing gave me the drive to leave and press on without looking back. It is hard to believe that the past can sometimes haunt you, and it can also prohibit you from living life to the fullest without any regrets or pain.

On January 19, 2001, I lived in an apartment complex with my daughter, who was 3 years old at the time, and had family that lived within a few miles. That can be a wonderful thing in many ways, but it can also come with a host of problems. I got to witness my aunt, who was 33 years old at the time, across the way from my apartment, experiencing a life of domestic violence. She had broken loose from children's father that had only been released from jail about a year before on a malicious wounding charge against her. She was in a new relationship and was moving on with her life. On any other day in any other life, that should have been a positive.

It was two days before my daughter's fourth birthday, and I needed to go out. My life was chaotic and I needed the pressure released any way I could. I walked my daughter over to my aunt's and my younger cousins' apartment. I knew she was wither her cousins for the evening and she would be fine. My friend, Peaches, came over to my house and I had already taken a shot of alcohol. I swear I was not really a drinker at this point, so the one shot was doing a number on me and my friend. She was already making me another drink. I was looking to do something fun in the dark place where I found my life at that point. This was how I had chosen to handle the pressure that night, and the night was just starting.

A couple of hours had passed as I was finishing getting ready and feeling the effects of my one drink, there was a hard knock at the door. The continuous knocks got harder and harder. I was starting to feel the effects of the alcohol and was preparing to fix my second drink. My friend answered the door. My cousin came through the door in a state of helplessness and all she could say was, "Momma been shot." Every kid in that house was under fourteen. There were her three daughters and my 3 year old daughter. I just stood there in place, numb and unmoving. For a split second I zoned out in a state of shock. But I was grateful at the same time that none of the kids had been hurt, including my daughter. The drink and the news were doing the job of washing all the "good" feeling out of me.

"Call 911."

I'm not a hundred percent sure if it was my voice or someone else's, but I just handed off my cordless phone for someone else to dial. "Come on. Come on. Let's go."

As I went outside with my cousin, who had just delivered the news that her mother had been shot several times, the neighbors were already gathering in the space between our complex and other units. The sound of *pop, pop, pop … pop … pop* had brought them outside to inquire what the commotion was all about. The door to my aunt's place was open and the kids were all out. One of them was holding my little daughter and from her face, I could see she was in a daze. I had no idea what was going through her young mind in that moment, but she does not seem to remember that day now - and I thank God for that. I was in no place to be a real comfort for her in that moment and my night wasn't over yet.

While I was getting ready for my night out, my daughter was sitting with my cousins in my aunt's living room watching a movie. They had heard a knock at the door. My aunt was in the kitchen, so one of the kids went to the peephole to check, as they had been taught to do. The middle child had recognized her Daddy and had no way of knowing or understanding that he shouldn't be let inside anymore.

He entered the house and rounded the corner to the kitchen where my aunt was coming to see who was there.

She said, "You need to leave."

He walked her backward around the corner with the threat of his presence and the belief that he was going to convince her of what he wanted or else.

She stayed strong and said, "I want nothing more to do with you."

The kids were still watching their movie, gathered on the sofa on what might have been the last normal moment in some of their lives.

He was long gone by the time I walked inside.

I couldn't go around the corner. The way he had shot her several times, the place where she was standing inside the kitchen but still near the doorway, and how she fell while he kept shooting her had sent her blood splattering across the dining room wall. I saw that and I could not make it around the corner to see the rest of it.

She was still alive.

The ambulance had come while I stood frozen by the sight of blood splatter on the wall. I clung to the wall to find protection from it all and refused to go around that last corner. As the paramedics went in to try to save her, my mother and my grandmother arrived. As the family decided to follow behind and go to the hospital, I decided to go out to the bar with my friend. There is no pride in how I spent that night. I told my mom that I just couldn't go and see my aunt like that. I couldn't take it. I don't know for sure how much my family saw through me in that moment, but they let me get away with it. I went out just as I had planned, my first drink warm in my belly, and a trauma on my heart as an excuse to keep drinking.

I stepped out of my life, with all its violence, and I didn't have a care in the world. I wanted to be in a dream, and I was using every drop of liquor I could get to make that happen.

In the town where we lived, the nightlife ended around twelve or twelve-thirty. My friend took me to the hospital. It was time to face the fact that my aunt was shot and fighting for her life.

The waiting area outside of the trauma unit was full of family and friends. The family pastor was there for comfort. I walked into this intense, emotional scene buzzing from a night of heavy drinking. It was more than I had ever drunk before.

As I tried to keep calm and settled, I insisted to go and see her. Her eyes were closed and the respirator and heart monitor filled the room with those noises that mark the line between life and death.

I took her hand and begged. "Please, tell me you're all right. Squeeze my hand."

And she did.

I told her, "You cannot die. You have young daughters who look up to you and need you. I promise you it will be all right. Squeeze my hand, if you understand."

I waited and was about to let go when she squeezed my hand again. I let her hand go and left the room to go back and tell my family what had happened. My aunt was still alive and she was still fighting.

As I walked up the hall toward the waiting room, I heard that noise. It was the long, drawn-out, piercing beep that cannot be ignored. As I kept facing forward and walking, everyone else in there was running past me and around me toward my aunt's room. The nurses and doctors were shouting instructions at each other and I was in denial that something went wrong.

The reality drained out of that moment and I was left trying to keep my feet walking up a surreal hallway in some other universe.

Once I made it back to my family, all I could whisper was, "Something has happened."

I had nothing else to offer that night. I stood there on my toes rocking back and forth, barely keeping my balance with the weight of everything on my shoulders and the buzz of the poisons running through my body.

The doctor came out and whispered into my grandmother's ear. Her distress look on her face told the entire room everything there was to know.

I felt numbness travel up and fill my legs. The dream world that I had been looking for crashed through on top of me and I fell backwards. A nurse was behind me and caught me as I almost blacked out.

The vague memory I have after that is being wheeled out of the hospital in a wheelchair to the car.

I didn't want to be my aunt.

If this story weren't true, if it were fiction, this would be the moment I turned my life around and straightened out the crooked edges. But it is not fiction. In real life, you can be going up and down at the same time. One can take a risk to get away from a bad place, but still being going down a dark path. I began a journey into my struggles even as I made an effort to escape abuse.

I moved away from my hometown. To keep from looking like I was stealing my daughter out of her father's life, I left her with my mother. I also needed to get my life in order before I brought her back into it. It turns out that it was good that I did.

I moved an hour away at first, but decided that was not far enough. So I moved again and this time it was four hours away. I got a job, but hadn't got my own place yet. It had not occurred to me that you needed a couple weeks of work experience before they would consider renting a place to you. I had thought a long-term hotel would work, but resort areas are seasonal. As tourist traffic changes, so do the prices of the hotel rooms. I wasn't in a position to pay for a place to stay as prices went up and what money I did bring with me ran out. It wasn't long before I depleted my savings as well.

Pride would not allow me to go back home. It was not an option for me. I knew going back home would put me back to that place of feeling like a failure.

I found myself sitting in my car by the beach with darkness closing in on me in more ways than one. I considered whether I should call any of my coworkers and ask for a place to stay. I had just met them. That first night in the car I couldn't leave it running because the lights would stay on if I did. So, I sat in the driver's seat in case someone came up on me then I could have time to start it and drive away. I parked in a hotel parking lot so I wouldn't be quite as exposed or isolated.

By this point, it was October and it was starting to get cooler. Before I got to April again, it would be very, very cold sitting in that driver's seat.

I remember sitting in that seat looking up through the windshield at the stars and saying, "I never thought I'd be here." Ironically, I didn't feel afraid or terrified because I knew God was protecting me and watching over me, keeping me safe from any harm or danger. To this day, I get emotional about this part of my life. It wasn't emotions of pain or self –pity, but rather emotions of gratefulness and being thankful of where I am today in my life. If I was to tell someone today that I slept in my car for 7 months, they would probably look at me and say, "Yeah right".

While sleeping in my car, I could never get a good night's sleep. I was restless and broken. I never got down to the deep sleep where you can let go of exhaustion and let your brain dream through all the baggage in your life that needs sorting. It was always a situation of waking up and being alert of my surroundings and ready for trouble if it came my way. Then, I'd try to steal a little more rest sitting in the driver's seat. I was going nowhere and I had reached the place where the ocean met the land, but I stayed in the driver's seat pretending to still be in control while I tried to find rest that was not there in that place for me.

My place of employment had a shower and a gym. I'd get up early from not really sleeping anyway and go pretend like I was going to work out at 5am before the sunrise. I could grab a shower and go on with my day.

I went back home every weekend pretending like seeing my daughter was the real reason why, but really I was driving all those hours on Friday evening to sleep inside a warm home. I slept hard, like I was trying to save up a week's worth of rest. I'd go back Sunday night or Monday morning and start over again. At the time, I didn't have the courage to tell my mother my situation. My entire family always looked at me as someone who was independent, head strong and successful. Successful to me was being financially stable, but in their eyes it meant leaving a one horse town to go after my dreams and make something out of nothing.

My mother kept asking for my address to send me cards and I kept avoiding the question to the point that she had to know something was wrong. That is what you call a mother's intuition.

With $3.10, I could put together a survivor's meal at 7-Eleven which got me a Big Gulp, a hotdog, and bag of chips.

Humans become accustomed to a life of surviving until that is the best we can do and it takes all our energy to do it. Surviving replaces really living.

When rates dropped enough, I could get a room for a night when I saved enough money. It was one night inside, and then it was time to start over.

The turning point came on New Year's Eve, December 31, 2004. This was not the end of my hard journey because a real life rollercoaster can be going up and down at the same time. We can figure out a piece of the answer and still have no idea what we are doing. A turning point is the beginning of a new direction, but it means you still haven't started the hard business of climbing up the mountain out of a very low place – you just finally see the mountain and know what needs to come next if you want to climb up.

As I spent my New Year's Eve cold and in my car, looking up at the same stars as before, I said, "This is not where I'm supposed to be."

This may seem so obvious to someone on the outside looking back at that woman shivering inside her car lonely and frightened, but she had to sit in the driver's seat at the end of that road for a long time before she realized it.

I was in the midst of a journey that passed through a very low, dark place. There was still a long way to go and a lot to experience before I asked, "Why me?"

It would be quite a while before I would be at the place to hear God answer, "Why *not* you?"

I had some things to learn before I would be reminded that I had a voice and a story to tell. I was ready to start living life instead of just surviving it.

I looked up through that windshield and teared up. I was so grateful and thankful. The tears reminded me of the emotions that I had built up and kept in as I displayed a tough exterior. I was ready to thank God for my life even though I was still shivering and sleeping in the driver's seat of my car and feeling like life was going nowhere. I was grateful that He had allowed me to continue to dream big and have hope that my situation was just temporary. Now, I was ready to start climbing out of the dark, low place and start living again.

It is not an easy journey, but I've been there, and I know the way out. Take my hand and know that you are not alone in this.

Why not you? Why not right now?

CHAPTER 3: PAINKILLERS AND LIVING IN BETWEEN

This is not easy for me. Taking this raw look into my life and past is frightening. I discussed it with my family, and I prayed. They were supportive and encouraged me to go forward. If anything about my story is going to help, I have to take an honest, powerful look at how I came out of the places where I found myself.

After the death of my aunt, and before I found myself in my car on the beach, I was in a place in between. I stopped in that in between place about an hour from the home and life I was trying to leave behind. Life is full of in-betweens that are meant to just be pauses in the action, or temporary setbacks; but we end up parked in those spots for longer than we intended. Instead of being a break from who we are, they become the spots that define who we are. We can get stuck and sink deep into the in-betweens. Days become weeks, which grow into months, which may become long years of surviving between life and something else. We might grow from having struggled there and finally escaped from there, but very few people grow for staying there.

After my aunt was buried, I went through a phase where I went numb. Nothing could phase me and nothing anyone said or did could hurt me. Part of my struggle would come from my desire to be and stay numb because feeling everything else was too much.

I realized that it was my time to move. One hour away from my baby's father might be the difference between life and death for me. Everything I saw across the way that led to my aunt's end was mirrored in my life. The jealousy and abuse filled my relationship and therefore filled my days and life. I saw my life going the same way it went for my aunt, if I stayed.

My mother loved me and sought to help me; she suggested that I leave my daughter with her as I went to do what it was I needed to do. I know many of you reading this maybe can't imagine leaving your daughter behind with someone as you moved on. It was not an easy decision for me as I went to my in-between place, but it was a decision based on desperate reason. I was in my early twenties and, though not long ago in total years, I was a different person at that point. Now, on this side of the struggles that young mother would face, I believe that I needed time to myself. I was also a loose cannon. If pushed the wrong way, I could go off in more than one bad way. I thank God for having a supportive mother who was willing to help me whenever she can.

Then, there was the fear. My biggest fear at that moment of leaving was "what if he finds me?" If I left my daughter in the safety of my mother's home in the same town as her father, he would not be motivated to come track me down for taking her away. At that moment, it seemed the most logical and sane choice. It seemed the safest choice for us all to go on living. And unfortunately at that point in my life, away from me was safer for my little girl than with me. I was scared to go on living in that place. I could not imagine meeting someone new and waiting to see how the anger and jealousy would drive the man I wanted to escape. I had already seen up close exactly what could happen.

An hour away from home and an hour beyond the life I wanted to leave behind, I got a job at a healthcare facility as an HR associate. I had coworkers that were all going through their own motions in life. They each had some type of chaos in their life. There were divorces, trouble with children, depression, and more.

During our smoke breaks outside, I learned that they were all coping with medication. I was from a small town; this notion that you could just go to the doctor and get something to deal with the feelings life gives you was entirely new to me.

Before I go on with my story, I want to make one clear note. This chapter is not meant to in any way imply that people should never take medication for anxiety or depression. There are people with real, diagnosed conditions that need to be on medication for themselves and others in their lives. There is no shame in that and there is no shame in seeking help when it is needed. Under proper supervision, these types of medication are useful tools for facing life with some otherwise debilitating and sometimes dangerous conditions. Please do not take my story as a call to go off medication that is properly prescribed, monitored, and used responsibly. My story is dealing with a different kind of use for these medications.

One of my coworkers during one of those discussions told me to "try one." She gave me my first Xanax. I'm not sure if I took it or it took me. I felt like jelly. I was relaxed and unbreakable. A person could have given me their worst in that moment and it would have been like nothing to me. I found my numb and then some. From that moment of feeling the numb instead of everything else, it "worked."

The problem was that I had to come back to work the next day. All the anxiety, depression, fear, and stress came with me. They felt that much more intense and that much heavier for knowing that a pill could melt them away for me for a little while.

Over the next couple of months, I lived in a world where people said, "Take this" and I did.I finally reached a point where I had enough sense to at least say, "Let me go to the doctor."

The doctor heard me out and agreed that I was suffering from depression and anxiety. I was started on anti-depression meds, running through trials on Zoloft, Paxel, and others. They experiment with you to figure out what works and at what dosage, but I had already been taking meds randomly before all this too.

One weekend on the highway, on my way back to see my daughter, a tractor trailer truck raced past me. Anxiety I was still feeling changed to the feeling of my chest caving in. I was short of breath, and I had to pull over to the side of the road not knowing what was going on.

I called my doctor who said, "You're having an anxiety attack."

I was instructed to find a bag in my car and to take deep breaths.

We switched medication again and then I couldn't sleep on top of everything else. So, we added more medication on top of that to help me sleep. I was taking Zoloft before work, a Xanax during the day, and something else to help me sleep at night. It took three in a row through the day to make me feel normal and all the while the combination was pushing me up and down at the same time. I was being squeezed in the place in-between where I was just trying to live.

To try to deal with this squeeze, I was still going out to drink socially, adding alcohol to this mix in my body. I was adding hurt, guilt, and shame as I tried to combine all these chemicals to deal with hurt, guilt, and shame. These were all the things I didn't want to face.

This became my continuous cycle. This was my new normal, everyday. I was getting refills on a constant basis and getting my dosage upped as well.

We went out as coworkers on lunch break and I started having a drink with my meal in the middle of the day.

It was during those hours at home by myself that my better angels tried to break through all of this new normal. I was going down to my car and I said, "Something is missing."

A part of me considered going back home away from this environment and a bigger part of me wanted to do just that; but, I had a thick layer of pride in the way. My mother always thought I would be a great success and have it together. I didn't want to let her or my family down. I certainly did not want them to see what I had become living in-between life and something else. My pride was so strong, and I could not bring myself to ask to go home.

I ignored the signs that day and let the opportunity of that moment of clarity to pass. I did ask God what was missing, but I ignored any answer He might have given.

I started hanging out more and partying more. In many ways, I was living like a teenager again and trying to take the chance to live out all that I might have missed by becoming a mother so young.

If you hang out in the clubs long enough and often enough, you get known by the people that are there. I got a similar version of normal there that I had experienced with my coworkers in the form of, "Try this."

I tried marijuana and my response was, "I like that."

From about age twenty-one in 1999 through 2004, I engaged in a five year period of the in-between living of a pain killing and a pain hiding lifestyle. The best summary of that time period is that I should have been dead and it is no small miracle that I came out of it at all. Sometimes small miracles are more than enough. I consider it a miracle and a blessing that I never used any hard drugs. If hard drugs or any other form of pain killer is your drug of choice in between normal life, we need to help you find your way out too. Since you are still alive and reading this, you have the small miracle you need to get out of this place.

I was in that environment where everyone did something, so normal was a really bad thing that no one was in a place to recognize.

I couldn't eat. For three days, I couldn't eat. With the help of my doctor, I realized the mess of stuff I was using to keep my new normal included marijuana, which gave me the munchies. Without it, my body did not have the same desire to keep eating.

In addition, I did not want to leave the house. I remember pulling up to the Wal-Mart and seeing all the people. I felt the world closing in to crush me, and I just drove back home.

My doctor referred me to a psychiatrist. Everyone is entitled to their opinions on this profession, but there is a big problem with a culture that discourages seeking help. Whether it is from the church, trusted family, rehab, or professionals of some other kind, it is called help for a reason. Not seeking help is part of societal shaming, and shaming will kill you. Decisions have consequences and the decision to stay in your new normal instead of seeking out help can have very serious consequences – miracle killing consequences.

I found myself on the couch sharing my problems. My psychiatrist said a beautiful thing to me. "It's a mental thing. This is not you – not who you are. You have moved into a dark place trying to escape and you are still not happy. I need you to do something for the next ten days. Every morning, look at yourself in the mirror and give yourself a five minute motivational speech. Give it like you are telling it to someone else you are trying to help. You will get out of this darkness, get your daughter back, and get out of this funk."

The first two days I tried it, this did not work. I felt as stupid doing it as some of you feel hearing it, I'm sure. After three or four days, my mindset did start to change and that was the point. No matter what path out of the darkness a person tries, mindset is a big part of it. Along with other factors and support systems, mindset is the key between success and failure. Thinking positive doesn't solve everything, but thinking negative works every time in the other direction.

This changed my life. I still had a long journey and plenty more mistakes ahead of me, but I was ready to stop the same, old mistakes.

My job was not helping, and I knew this.

I finally said, "I have to get out of this situation."

The stress of trying to meet my sales quota and everything else that went with that work environment were my pile of excuses to keep doing what I was doing to deal with it.

"I have to quit," I realized.

I'm not suggesting everyone go out and quit their jobs to relieve their stress. As a stress reliever, that may not be the best plan for obvious reasons. Don't let your job or anything else be your anchor of excuses to drag you down where you drown in the darkness. A job is food, rent, health insurance, and week-to-week survival. All jobs and all life come with stress. Running from stress is not a solution because you will always be running toward new stress. But you have to take a cold, honest look at the things that make up normal in your life. It may be family, friends, work, or the places you go, but if your normal is a dark place where you are surviving in the in-between place masking your pain instead of living, you may need to make the hard choice of cutting yourself free of those heavy anchors, once you figure out which ones are dragging you under. In some ways, dealing with the toxic environment of the job may be the trickiest of those fixes. We need a job. If your current job is part of what is killing you, being dead with benefits isn't much use.

I gave my thirty-day notice on January 1, 2004, making the 31st my last day. My notice was listed as "due to medical reasons." I was ashamed to go into any more detail than that.

My employer denied the benefits and I went to my doctor to address the issue and get the proper forms filled out. I went for five months with no money coming in. I had saved some and borrowed where I could. I got by. Finally, the State of Virginia awarded me back pay of $8000 and I was able to move on.

My story wasn't done and still isn't. This is just one part in a long journey. There are triggers to go back. Things in life come in at full force and there is a temptation to smoke something, to drink something, or to go back to pills. The desire to kill our pain is human nature. I would love to say something won't come along to trigger me back into that place, but I can't because I deal with anxiety to this day. New stages of life, including my daughter graduating and dealing with the separation anxiety, come up now. There are responsible uses for medication under the proper supervision, but you also need a support system in place and you need to be able to seek help when it is needed and even when it just might be needed.

Pills aren't the only form of painkiller though.

People in my life then and now were causing pain and possibly leading me into places that could kill me. Relationships can cause severe emotional pain, which can be the root of seeking to be numb and fighting to hold onto normal. Friendships can be the source and you have to get rid of the painkillers.

Let go of the toxic people that are serving as a hindrance or a roadblock in your life.

I was pursuing an acting career and song writing professionally at one stage of my life. Anything creative in life can be subject to attack by people that don't understand or don't like seeing someone else pursuing a dream. People can be driven to pull you down on purpose or just because that is who they are. They come along and ask you to join them in getting high, going to one happy hour after another, or pulling you away from the dedicated work that goes into finding success with any creative, positive pursuit.

My family, I love them, but I could not tell them everything. There was negative energy there and misunderstanding about what I wanted to accomplish at different points and why.

We worry so much about what other people think and change our lives to accommodate those people in ways that lessen who we are and what we want to be – what we should be.

At some point, that type of life will always be less and always be darker and always be stuck in the shadows between instead of what it was meant to be until we decide it only matters what God thinks. Only God judges me and only His judgment is clear. Others that want to judge us are looking out of their version of the new normal. That type of judgment will never take us to a good place. It will never help us become what we were meant to be.

Trying to fit in kills and steals your joy. Their words work you down.

I have been in relationships with guys that were physically and emotionally abusive. That changes who you are and holds you down from becoming who you are meant to be.

I've stayed when I was called "nothing" or a "bitch." Words are powerful. We lie to ourselves and pretend we can stand up under them, but if we stay with those painkillers, we give them and their words the power.

I would pretend to go to the bathroom and I would just cry and bawl from those words. I remember being in the back of his car just praying to have my happiness back. Happiness is my sanity and without it the walls are closing in.

How many of you get sick and tired of being sick and tired? You're stuck in a rut and it seems like it is not going to get any better. Just know everything you go through is temporary and a life lesson. We can't let our past keep blocking our brighter future. Don't allow your limitations to cloud your vision. If you have a goal or achievement you want to accomplish and need validation, go to God in prayer for confirmation. Not only will He reveal things to you but will use people or situations to give you affirmation.

In life we tend to worry about others and how they will feel when we act on a creative idea. At the end of the day, you can't please everybody. And remember that not everyone who you think may be happy for you has your best interests in mind or heart. It's foul but true. If you are continuing to find your purpose, reflect back over your life to see what worked and didn't work for you. What was or is still your passion? Remember that your passion is usually formed around your purpose. You may have a passion to sing or to be a professional athlete or to pursue some talent within you. Your God given talents will showcase your purpose according to His will.

Your happiness is your sanity. Don't steal it from yourself by just surviving your life in between where you were and where you should be going. Don't allow others to steal your life with their negativity and discouragement. Don't allow the devil and his demons to steal your soul through bad choices. Don't cover it over by filling your life with painkillers.

CHAPTER 4: BREAKING FREE FROM CHILDHOOD PAIN

It took me until I got into my 30s to finally come to grips with the truth that I could no longer be a victim from what I went through in my past during my younger days. This is not to say that those experiences don't matter, it is not to excuse anyone who has hurt me or caused pain in my life, and it is not pretending that certain things never happened to me. I know there are many reading this who went through far more for far longer than I did. We each carry the pain of our own experiences and we can only deal with our own suffering. Those experiences on a child or young woman have impact that is felt deep into adulthood. There is no ignoring that. What I am saying is that we are not served by living in that pain and sacrificing our futures by carrying it with us without relief. It must be confronted and addressed or it will rule our lives. We will sacrifice our lives to being a victim of those experiences. For ourselves, those that love us, and for God, we owe it to him to take the steps to be free of that pain. We deserve a life.

It does not serve me to live in excuses for my behavior and the choices throughout my life. I can trace a map through my life of anger, resentment, pain, and poor choices. Those that get close to me feel these things in my life too. It gets worse when I'm under stress or going through struggles. I don't want to live like that or give off that negative energy in my life any longer.

Some of you have lived through abuse at different points in your life, including as children. Whether abused younger or older in life, it plays a part in who you have become. It plays into where you go in life. It shades your choices. It does not have to dictate your future from this point forward and this does not have to define who you are. It is not your identity and you can choose not to be a victim of it any longer.

I know when I was somewhere between 8 and 10 that I was being touched in a way that was uncomfortable to me. It was someone in our neighborhood, which helped in his getting away with it. A child does not know how to feel about these situations. The fear and confusion set in and take root over time. It hangs with us and grows as we go through life. Even as adults, when we understand better what was happening, we have a much deeper set of negative emotions to extract by the time we are in a position to deal with them. It may take help to get these things untangled from your adult life, but it is worth setting yourself free.

Who do you tell as a kid though? Because I didn't know who to tell or how to say it; I just didn't say anything to anyone up until I wrote this. That's too long. Then, I asked myself if this was just what normal was. I asked what I had done to deserve this – to bring it onto myself.

When I was 13 or 14, the danger resurfaced. This was the late 70s and early 80s, so the education to know to tell and how to tell wasn't there. This was the era of keeping your mouth closed about such things. We didn't have the same support system in that time that is available today. Back then, I could be beat with a yardstick until bruises showed, but protective services would be involved today. When my mom and dad argued, things could get ugly, but what goes on in the house stays within the family. That's how it was and that's how it still is in many places now.

I was out of school and old enough to stay in a house on my own. While my grandma worked, I stayed at her house. A family friend used to come over to use the phone because he didn't have one. Even then, I was instructed to not let in anyone that I didn't know, but I knew him and he came over often when family was there. He came to use the phone that day because he knew I was there alone.

I didn't think anything of it and just let him inside. He was 7 or 8 years older than me and out of school.

I was watching television in the living room. Across the wall of my grandma's house above the television was a big mirror, so I could see into the kitchen behind me. I was aware something was wrong early into the visit. He was claiming to carry on a conversation and acting it out, but I saw his hand was holding down the receiver on the wall phone so that no one was on the other end of the line at all. He was looking at me as he pretended to speak on the phone.

Something wasn't right. I felt the danger.

I got up and turned around just as he was putting the chain on the front door.

"What are you doing?" I tried to show maturity and strength, but I was scared inside.

He said, "I just want to talk."

I thought and prayed over and over. *Don't let him hurt me.* I know thousands upon thousands of others have prayed the same thing over the years. I know many did not get the answer they asked for. Hurting children is a horrific act that goes on every day around the world. Many, many people live with those emotional and spiritual scars into their adulthood. Some live with the physical scars too. There is evil in the world. There is also a God that sees and is in control of the universe. I cannot explain why evil is given a place in moments like this and I would not dream of lecturing someone who has gone through abuse about that, but I will say that God extends grace and he offers healing. I believe it to the core of my being still, and I claim those gifts now.

I made up a lie that day. "My great aunt is expecting me."

"No, she's not. Let's talk – just talk."

"No, I'm serious," I said. "She told me to come over and I told her five minutes. She'll call and then she'll come over here mad at me for not coming like I said to give her medicine. I need to go over there to take care of that and then I can come right back."

Guardian angels were on the scene because he opened the door and let me out.

I sat over at my great aunt's house for a while. I still did not tell her why; I just sat at the window and watched my grandma's house. I think it finally dawned on him that he was just sitting in someone else's house and I was not coming back. He finally left.

I waited until everyone got off work and then went back to my grandma's house.

I finally said something to my mom about it, but not enough to communicate the full danger I had felt. I more downplayed it in a sense as at the point I was more worried about getting in trouble because I answered the door. She spoke to my dad and really can't recollect what came out of it. After a few days, it was easy enough for the guy to talk his way out of any suspicion.

I should have said something when I was 8. One of my aunt's male friends played hide and seek with me. He asked me to turn cartwheels and his behavior was totally off. He was touching too long and leering in an odd manner. I didn't tell anyone. I never shared it.

Many go through things they never discuss. It lingers on into adult life. It plays a part in who we allow ourselves to become and the choices we make because of who we think ourselves to be.

As I went through being homeless, dealing with bankruptcy, and other struggles, I kept things to myself. I made my choices and I didn't talk to anyone about it. I had made a deep set pattern of hiding what was happening to me. I sunk deeper in because of who I had decided to be.

I can no longer live as the victim. It does not and has not worked for me.

My advice is that if you have gone through anything like this and it is too painful to face on your own, seek help in that process. You don't know how it will affect you opening that back up, but leaving it closed keeps you the victim. We blame ourselves and beat ourselves down no matter how much we know on the surface that this wasn't our fault. Getting free of it takes some work and that work sometimes requires help. Seek help. I no longer want to be held hostage by it and I don't want you to be either.

CHAPTER 5: OPPORTUNITY COMES WITH OPPOSITION

With every real opportunity in life, opposition follows. If opportunity is at the door or knocks on the door, then when you open it, opposition sneaks in through a window to get in your way. You can be surprised by this every time or you can be prepared to face it as a natural part of opportunity.

It was an unusual opportunity that lifted me out of being homeless and brought me to where I am now. My redemption would come in time, but it was a process, it involved timing, and I believe God's hand was on it through the victories and the setbacks.

I added to my homelessness some medical issues. I started to be in discomfort because of my hernia and top of depression which I hid very well. This is not the sort of thing one looks for in a blessing or an opportunity, but it turned out to be part of a bigger plan to move me where I needed to be.

My doctor at the time recommended me to have outpatient surgery. Repairing this umbilical hernia that I was born with would aid in having a normal belly button and no longer having any further discomfort. As a contractor at Verizon I could no longer keep my job. I hadn't been in the role long enough to justify a reason for them to hold it. I had to go back home. I didn't want to, but I was driven there by a circumstances beyond my control. As a contractor, I was not entitled to benefits either. So, home I went.

I was miserable at home. I felt like a failure having to backtrack all my steps to return there to heal. I was driven back there by forces outside myself and outside all my efforts to control life. I was looking for my great opportunity and I was in no place to realize this might be part of it. All I wanted to do was to leave that negative energy again.

I was still not facing that I had driven myself to a dead end trying to control my destiny without a purpose. All my money went to survival. I was simply making ends meet trying to earn enough for a night in a room here or there.

Still, it didn't feel right – none of it. It wasn't right living in my car obviously, but it wasn't right being back in my parents' house either.

My mom was happy to have me back, and God bless her for all of it. She didn't want to see here daughter out there in the open exposed and on the street. Mom felt at ease having me under her roof to see me through my healing.

I had this drive inside me to go. I saw complacency in friends and family all around me, and I had to escape. I saw what I thought at the time was my vision of my life going downhill had I stayed. People all through my life have pointed out that I could just stay with my parents and cut my expenses away. God blessed me with talents though and in the end, my talents are not staying under my parents' roof. It bothers me not to use my talent. It hurts deeply.

I prayed every day through my recovery about it. I felt I was taking five steps forward only to take ten steps back. I was right back in the same spot again.

It was during this time that my uncle bought a house out in the Washington D.C. metro area. He knew my medical situation and knew I was unhappy. He proposed that I could rent the finished basement from him. I'd have my own space, bathroom, and entrance for a reasonable rent. He knew I didn't have a job and he offered me a couple of months to get on my feet before I started paying rent.

It was an opportunity. My mom wanted me to stay and heal though.

With this and many situations in life, it is not wise to pass up the right opportunities. Don't let those key moments pass you by. Even if you are not sure, you still go after it.

This was a chance to strike out again on my own, but with a roof over my head. I would still have some family within reach.

Sadly, I still wasn't ready for my daughter. I was still in my twenties and certainly had not gotten my life together yet. I needed to get a job up there. I had to feel the area out. If it wasn't comfortable, safe, and a positive environment, there was no need to move my little girl into a bad situation.

My mom was fine with keeping her and supportive of my efforts. She hadn't fulfilled her dreams in life. Not only had she had a child young also, but she was only thirteen when she had my brother. She let me go after my dreams and she got attached to my daughter. Even though I knew I was and should be a parent, I was still ready to live my twenty-year-old life.

Now I know better. I am a parent first, but that's not who I was at the point in my growth as a person.

Still, leaving her again was a tough decision. It gave peace at home. There was peace with her father. She had family around. I came to see her every other weekend during that time or whenever I could. It was not an easy time in my story as a mother.

I did get exposed to different cultures moving out of the country town to Washington D.C metro area.

Five years into that life, I was able to experience life, networking, and the history of that city. Something was missing. I had the roof, I had contact with family, I had various circle of friends, and I had some time with my daughter. I had a good job, and I was independent. But I wasn't complete.

I wasn't seeing it. I still wasn't satisfied

It took my boyfriend at the time to tell me. "You don't have your daughter here."

It didn't dawn on me before that. God was telling me that I had it together. I had a system of support. Now I was ready to get my child. It's time.

I made contact with my parents and explained this choice to them. This came with some trouble. In my daughter's eyes, living with grandma and grandpa was normal. She had family in town. I came into her life every other weekend or for special events. This was her normal from an early age.

I didn't want her to pass into her teenage years and on through to a young woman like this. The respect level and any chance at real connection would be gone. The resentment would come and fill her life. It would shape her as a person.

She was twelve or thirteen at this point and the transition was going to be a fight. In my phase of life at that point, she had gone from eight to twelve. She was attached to my parents.

I come in and tell them, "I think I am ready now."

I had friends with kids at this stage and my situation with my daughter living away no longer made sense. Unless I was a person unfit to raise her, I needed to raise her. It was an obstacle. The opposition to this opportunity came in the form of lack of support for this decision. My family wanted to keep things the way they were.

I took a lot of flak for wanting to uproot her. I felt resentful for that response too. My feeling was "Don't you want me to step up and be the parent."

They understandably had their doubts in my decision. I couldn't explain or justify the choice to not step up and be the parent I was supposed to be any longer.

My mom kept running the scenarios though. What happens if you oversleep and you're running late and you forget about getting her to school? What do you do if you have to go to work, but she misses the bus? What do you do if she gets sick? How will you handle that without family around like we have down here? This went on and on and on.

My daughter's dad and his mom weren't buying it either.

Everyone was hung up on it being four and a half hours away.

I had something to prove at this point. I felt I shouldn't have to, but now I did.

It was a good time, but it was sad too. I cried at night. I doubted my decision often.

I prayed about my doubts. God came back with challenging me on why I would question getting what I asked for. Any time we go for what God has planned, people are going to question and challenge. Opposition will come.

I will never forget the day I took her. You would have thought I was talking her to another country or another planet even instead of just up the road. Everyone was crying and making a huge deal. From my standpoint, I wanted everyone to settle down and support my decision and my step forward.

I didn't understand the full scope of it. My daughter was filling a void for my family – especially for my mom and our relationship. I was stealing normal from all of them at that moment.

I was closed off growing up and not prone to share my thoughts or feelings with family the way I can do now with others. I'll tell a stranger first before family or even friends. Family and friends are in a position to judge me. I won't share it for that reason.

The relationship between me and my mother was tolerable then. I respected her and she supported me, but the connection kind of stopped at that tolerable level. My daughter provided some of these missing pieces of connection for my mother. I thank my mother for building that connection with my daughter when I was not able and failed to do so. Thank God for my mother or there may not have been a chance to recover the relationship with my daughter. For all I lived through, my mother did the work to keep that opportunity alive for me whether she realizes that or not. I couldn't be more grateful.

Having kids at an early age is a life changing challenge. Girls become mothers while they still are a kid themselves. A person that becomes a mother too young still wants to be out with peers doing what young people do. I thank God that my mother stepped in when I was still this person because so many kids in this situation don't have that. Her wisdom may have saved us both.

I wasn't ready when I had my daughter. This is a truth that is tough for me to face even looking back on these events now. I was dumb and in love. I was so far away from ready. A little age comes with a whole different mindset and level of maturity. You think differently. You even dress differently.

As the person I am now, I dress and behave classy for my daughter. She is watching and these things communicate values and character. It communicates how I value myself and how she will value herself. It is a far bigger deal than many young mothers realize.

These experiences shaped who I am and were used by God to build the person He wanted me to be. Even still, if I could go back to the young girl that was me or any others like me, I would tell them to stay away from the choices that lead to becoming a young mother. Life is worth more than the life changing mistakes that come too early.

By the time I got my daughter and moved her with me to D.C., building that relationship as a true parent was challenging. The first six months were hell. She didn't like anything about it. The adjustment for both of us was enormous. She cried, lashed out, and was outright disobedient to me. I questioned myself and my choice often. She wanted to pack her bag and head back to my mother's house. I considered allowing it.

Friends who had become successful parents told me, "You are her mom. This is part of it. This is how kids treat you. You have to become the mom now."

I was used to being by myself and for myself. Now I had less freedom. I had a responsibility to be there and be sure food was on the table.

After that, she came around. She made friends. I supported her through the struggle of the transition and beyond. I helped her adjust to a different culture. In our small, country town, people were either black or they were white. In D.C., there was a mix of cultures from all over the world.

Today, she is a beautiful woman. She is graduating this year and her life is full of promise that me and my mother missed out on because we had become mothers so young. She made better choices and avoided many of our mistakes. That is a blessed thing to be able to say as a parent. It warms and redeems my soul.

We did it. We made it.

If she had graduated down there, I would have attended, but it would be different. She would have grown up in a different environment, raised by her grandparents, with a part-time mother that would not take her in, and she would carry that in her heart. There is no telling what kind of trouble that might have driven her toward in her life.

The memories would be different for both of us. I would have been there for some, but not nearly all major events. I would have missed most important moments. I would have missed every tiny moment and experience in between too. I got to be there for the struggles, the choices, the victories, the jobs, and the life. I'm thankful I chose to take the opportunity for the life we do have now despite all the opposition that opportunity demanded that I face.

Opportunities don't come easy. There is a window of opposition behind the door. That's how it is and how it must be faced. It does not come by luck. There is a destiny beyond the opportunities.

Opposition comes. It always does. You must be prepared to face it. It is the price that must be paid to reach the reward beyond the door. Pray. Encourage yourself. Find the support to strengthen you as you work to take the opportunities that are yours. They represent the life you could have which is filled with the moments that belong to you and the people you love.

CHAPTER 6: ONLY GOD CAN JUDGE

I found myself in a little bit of a bind and needing assistance. I never wanted public aid because I had worked so hard during my life to take care of my own troubles and to face up to the consequences of my own choices. In my eyes, people on the system were folks who made bad choices and wanted someone else to fix them. I was looking through eyes of judgment because I was so hard on myself when I messed up.

So, I was sitting in the waiting room of the office where you go to apply for aid. I was dressed well, like how someone would dress for a job interview or any other professional meeting. I wanted desperately not to be associated with the type that would be in this situation of seeking help. It hurt me and it hurt my fragile ego.

I saw people living outside their means, and I was guilty of it too. One woman sat there with two kids, a baby in stroller, and pregnant with another. I felt like shaking my head. I had ended up with a daughter out of high school. My mother had my brother younger than that. I was not doing exactly what this woman was doing, but still, I placed myself in a position of judgment in that moment.

I saw my situation as temporary, so I judged my life to be different from those around me. It was difficult for me to swallow my pride and to face that I needed help, much less to go out and ask for it. Even as I judged, I did not want to be judged.

Only God can judge. We all do a fine job of trying to do that work for Him, but it is not our job. We all do it though. I spend much of my life trying to avoid the judgment of others and I still find times to pass judgment on others. Only God should judge.

In a world of judgment, we spend our lives living for others. That does not mean we are doing good deeds for others. It means that we are making our choices to try to please others and that is a formula for a disastrous life.

This is not what we are supposed to be doing with our lives. Focusing on the judgment of others is a distraction from our purpose. Judging others is a misuse of our purpose.

I always wonder what others think of me. I'm seeing myself constantly through their eyes physically, in relationships, and with the choices I make. I'm trying to validate others' opinions wondering what they will think.

I had moved to Washington D.C. with the idea of making a better living for myself and my daughter. My family had high expectations for me, and I felt like I had very little room to fail. There was no space to fail or be down with them watching.

As I made my way in the wealthy sections of D.C., people didn't seem to understand what it took for me to keep up a house, responsibilities, dealing with shutoffs, eviction notices, and still struggling with a lifestyle of poor decision making that I hadn't quite shaken loose from yet.

We all try this to some extent. We work hard to keep up with the "Joneses." I remember doing my best to put on a façade of having it all and having it all together. I had the appearance of a nice house. I was renting, but I had the appearance. I landed the nice job and fought to work my way up. But in that rich county, the richest in the world, you have to have two incomes to keep up those levels of appearance. I was still trying to pull it off anyway.

I, like many people, was living above my means. I was buying and buying just to showcase. And, I was struggling from paycheck to paycheck.

It was about six or seven years ago that I got the eviction notice. Other times the lights got turned off. I was embarrassed and couldn't figure out a person in my life I could tell. This is not a "social friends" type of conversation. Those are the friends you are trying to keep the image up with that you still have it made.

I only told the guy I was dating, which stung a little because I am not the type that wants to depend on a man for support. He helped me out a little.

I swallowed my pride finally and sought out help with services in the community that I had always looked down upon. I used to get upset at people like "them" and then I found myself in the office with them, in my nice suit, seeking help.

To add to the pain to my ego, I was told that in the midst of my difficulty and need, I actually made too much money to get help. I wondered how far down did I have to get? If I ever reach the point to give back to the community in a substantial financial way, it will be a fund to help the average working family that hits a hard time. When they aren't poor enough to qualify for aid, I want to be able to help them over the bump in the road before it does get worse. In many areas, if you own your own house, you do not qualify for help no matter how bad the rest of your situation is. We push people toward the American Dream and then cut them loose it seems. One stumbling block can do a number on the average family.

I had to go find help another way. Still proud and still choking on my pride and need at the same time, I reached out where I could. I discovered a valuable network of churches that would help out with a bill or a grant to tide a person over, even if they did not attend the church. Through referral services, I was able to find a little help to see me through.

For me to be able to swallow my pride and ask for help means I've come a long way. It was a humbling experience and served to begin to teach me not the judge others in the same way that I sought and struggled not to be judged. One hard truth is that for others to be able to give as God calls us to do, those in need have to be willing to receive. Judgment and pride only serve to break down this giving that God intended for us to do.

CHAPTER 7: CONVICTED TO GROW

As I have been looking back on the life unfolding before me in the pages of this book, I feel convicted. That's not to say that I was feeling guilty over mistakes I've made or struggles I've been through. Those things have shaped me into who I am and who I am going to be as I continue to grow. My conviction was about my future and where my growth needs to go tomorrow.

I was convicted to list off my strengths and weaknesses; I was convicted to take a long, honest look at myself. This was not just for the purpose of seeing who I am now. I did this because I needed to have a vision of who I am becoming and who I am meant to be. My purpose requires me to grow out of my current state of comfort or stagnation. I need to see where I am meant to go next. I must understand what strengths will get me there and which weaknesses may be holding me back. I need to see the path for turning weaknesses into strengths.

I have worked in human resources at more than one company. This requires us to interview new applicants. One question we ask is for the candidate to list weaknesses. With a job interview, they tend to tell us what we want to hear. This question really needs to be asked of ourselves, about ourselves. That may be the only time that question is truly useful.

I didn't spring for dry erase/ white boards for this project. I went ahead and picked up ordinary poster boards and put them up in my garage. I wanted to see these lists every day when I left for work and every day when I came home. Again, this was not meant to make me feel guilty, nor to beat myself over the head, but to keep my growth in front of my eyes daily. I was convicted to grow and this was a part of that process for me.

We put on masks for the world and even for ourselves. We pull back on honesty with ourselves and with others. We flinch away from transparency. We don't want our flaws and mistakes exposed. Things we've been through shape us, but then we want to push them down and hide them from ourselves for a lot of reasons.

Everybody has some set of significant weaknesses and it is a strength to be able to face those and learn to grow despite them. Perfection would leave us no room for growth. Thank goodness we are not perfect. We might not like what our weaknesses say about us, but not being able to be honest about those things may be the greatest weakness of all.

As I listed off my weaknesses, this is what ended up on my poster board:

1. communication/ holding back
2. anxiety
3. self medication/drinking
4. overweight/ lack of healthy living
5. trusting others/ closing off
6. lack of commitment
7. procrastination

People on the outside don't know all these things about me. Some people in my life would be quite shocked by some of the things on this list. I mask my shortcomings well when I have to. This is why it is tempting to shy away from transparency - because we can hide some of these weaknesses for a time from some circles. The lies work for us, for a while. We can't grow from lies though. Lying to ourselves about these things can be the most damaging act of all.

Lack of commitment in particular is counter to my purpose. I have to finish what I start to meet my purpose, so this weakness is very important for me to know and face daily as I seek to grow.

I tend to lapse. I don't want to stand up under pressure. I have to create deadlines for myself to maintain my commitment to the things that matter in my life. I have to face this significant weakness head on.

My procrastination and difficulties with organization come from trying to juggle a dozen things at once. I need to focus on one thing at a time, even when life throws a million things at me at once - as life tends to do. We all have to develop the ability to multi-task, but that still requires the ability to take those multiple tasks and organize them so that you can focus on one at a time. In the end, you end up with dozens of open ended tasks that aren't finding completion, and that is not multi-tasking at all.

My grandmother has some deep, inner issues. I am much like her in a number of ways. Some of those ways I am proud of and others I have to watch. These issues are my excuse for drinking. I drink to wash over pain. I drink to address boredom. I drink to celebrate. I always have an excuse, if I want to drink.

My goal in putting these weaknesses before me is to self-evaluate every three months after facing them daily. I want to see where I am with them and what I need to do next.

I did the same thing with my strengths, and here is the list I came up with:

1. creativity

2. leadership skills
3. writing
4. speaking
5. acknowledging my weaknesses
6. a heart to help others/encouraging
7. determination/go getter
8. a relationship with God

My relationship with God may be positioned last on this list, but it is not last on the list in importance. It is a <u>significant</u> strength in the midst of my weaknesses. It is not a strength because I am strong or because I am so good, but it is a strength because that relationship shines through my weaknesses. This year alone, through my work writing this book and everything else I do, that relationship has carried me and is bringing me to a closer connection with Him.

My creativity fuels my writing and speaking. It refreshes my life and adds to everything with which I am involved. It comes in handy in small ways. We held an event with the women at church that I titled SWAP. It stood for Strutting With A Purpose. The catchy title built up excitement and brought deeper meaning to the activity. It is a small thing, but creativity adds to life through the small things.

I've had to serve as a leader within my professional life and outside it, too. There is a difference between just managing people and actually leading them. The fact that so many don't know the difference is why we have so few great leaders when we need them. Leaders empower people to do their best and to reach their purpose in life. Leaders lay out an example for others in big and small ways.

I do have a heart to give back. That is why I'm writing this book and laying my life out for others. That is why I use my writing and my speaking to lift up others. I particularly try to find ways to give back to other women. Those who are dealing with being single mothers, who are homeless, or who are struggling with some form of mental illness are quite dear to me. I have experiences that can help me relate to them and put me in a position to be able to reach out in a meaningful way.

It might seem like a contradiction to have determination as a strength while having procrastination and lack of commitment as weaknesses. But this is where this process pays off - by showing me exactly what I need to see. By seeing this strength and its potential in my life, it gives me a path to address those weaknesses and to grow beyond them. I do have a determination in my soul and with God's hand in my life, I can use that to overcome those weaknesses. I would have never seen that answer without being honest and putting my strengths and weakness out in front of my eyes like that.

Consider doing this for yourself and put them out to see daily. Find ways to grow in your strengths beyond your weaknesses. Gain a conviction toward growth so that you will do the hard work that comes with that process. Reevaluate every three months to see where you are and where you need to go next.

Don't share these things with everyone. They are not for just anyone. They are for you. Take yourself at face value and be transparent with yourself first. Turn those weaknesses into strengths.

We can't accept success without the process. There is a road to get there.

That visual motivation and transparent reminder is helpful – it is like a whisper from God. Every day, I walk into my garage and

I'm reminded of both my purpose and my process for getting there. Facing these things helps me to have a positive, uplifting attitude for myself and for others. This process turns conviction into action and action into growth.

CHAPTER 8: WRESTLING WITH TRUST

Trusting others is one of my weaknesses. It is possible to trust too easily, but my problem is the opposite. I withhold trust from others in my life. I tried to analyze why this weakness exists in my life and what it means. I've let past failures with people and relationships add a barrier in my life against future possibilities. I don't need to flip over to being one that trusts too easily, but I can't go on being one that does not trust at all – not if I want to really achieve my purpose in life.

My guard is up. Some people are secretive. I don't mean that people hide things exactly. By this I mean that people are selective with whom they share their business. By itself, this is not necessarily a flaw. We protect details about our finances and our relationships. I am one of those people. I do keep to myself in order to protect myself.

I realize that in the process of trying to keep my guard up and to keep my business safe and secretive, I have kept my circles small. When I was secretly homeless and living in my car, those people I called friends at my work went out of my life as soon as I moved. The same was true in each town where I lived. I kept my circles small while I was there and left those people behind each time I left. I did the same as I moved to D.C. Ninety percent of the people I knew when I first moved here have moved out of my circle since. Maybe it is more accurate to say that I moved them out as I moved on in my life.

I have to look at that and think I might be the common denominator as to why people are rotated out of my life so often and so easily. Some of it though is because of spiritual behavior. As I have grown out of old habits, I had to grow out of old friendships. I think God has positioned me to be around certain people at certain times in my life. I chose like-minded people as I was doing things that were unhealthy for my life and unproductive for my growth. As I chose to draw closer to God and to take positive action to improve my life and my situation, he orchestrated circumstances to move me on from certain relationships so that I would find like-minded people in my times of growth.

As I grew, I needed other things and other people. The challenge for me in my weakness though is to open myself up to trust God during these transitions and to trust the people He has put in my life for that growth. It is good to keep negative people out when you are trying to make positive change. It is not good to keep *everyone* out while trying to make positive change. Trust has a role in the growth and therefore closing off all avenues of trust closes off avenues of growth.

Wrestling with trust for a spiritual person is, in a way, wrestling with God. If we don't trust anyone in our lives, then we have to ultimately ask ourselves whether or not we trust God. If we fear that we will be hurt by the act of trusting to the point that we close ourselves off to it completely, then the person we really lack trust in is God Himself. We don't trust that He will protect us, we don't trust that He will heal us, we don't trust that He will pick us up, we don't trust that He is in control, we don't trust His timing, we don't trust His plan for our lives, or we don't trust Him to bless us.

Wrestling with God over blessings is not a new concept. In the Bible, Jacob wrestled with God at his moment of growth. He had made a mess of trust in his own life. He saw blessings as a thing to be stolen in life and he sparred with God to try to get a blessing. The way Jacob was living, he had to come to grips with the fact that his enemy was not his brother, his enemy was not his equally deceptive uncle, and his enemy was not even himself. He was living his life of distrust so that his real enemy was God. He was wrestling with God his whole life up to the point that he wrestled with God for real. Once Jacob lost his wrestling match with God, his name was changed to Israel and that's when he got his blessing. He did not get blessed because he bested God. He found blessing at God's hand because he finally gave up that struggle and really trusted God with his life for the first time in his life.

Beneficial people come into our lives to help us grow. If they are truly beneficial, it means that the relationship is mutually beneficial. A relationship that only provides benefit in one direction is not truly helpful to either party – not even the one receiving energy off the other. Growth in a relationship – any relationship – only comes when both are able to grow. Those mutually beneficial relationships are built on trust. These are the kind of people and the kind of relationships we have to surround ourselves with in life. We should look for these common traits of benefit and like-mindedness in the people we seek to trust.

This may be particularly challenging for women in the modern world mindset. The trust factor for us comes with a number of layers. It is true for many people, but I see in a lot of my female friends where baggage from childhood shapes our ability to trust each other. As modern as our society has become, there is still an old school layer of thought where the man is thought to be the head of the household. If I'm a single mother and have been throughout my adult life, then I'm the head in my life. My need to hold tightly to that is part of my baggage when it comes to trust. My daughter has joked that I'm too independent. Even in situations where a relationship is not necessarily trying to take away my role of being head of my life in all aspects, I still hold back and lock down my trust to try to protect myself in that regard.

In any romantic relationship in particular, I am quick to pop the brakes. I'm not comfortable letting someone too close to my heart, even if all indications are that they can be trusted. My past relationships are proving to be a hindrance to my future relationships. Relationships that could blossom, I end up cutting off short because of that fear and lack of trust.

I realized after enough years that I don't have to take certain things. I don't have to carry them around in my heart or on my shoulders any longer either. Many of us have been hurt over the years either physically, emotionally, sexually, or otherwise. We choose then to hide in our shells for fear of future hurts. I'll come out for a time, but I'm always ready to pop back into the shell to hide for whatever illusion of safety that hard shell around my life might provide.

Living like this, I'm very likely to let the right man go. I don't have to be in a relationship or be married to be complete, but I'm not doing myself any favors by living a life that is automatically closed off to that possibility. If I push every possibility away, then nothing is possible. That is not a healthy way to live.

Corporate America does not lend itself to trusting, open relationships. There is a dog eat dog approach to getting ahead. Politics, in and out of the work place, are designed to undercut trust or manipulate lives. The political world operates under the mantra of it's not what you know, but *who* you know. That sounds relational on the surface, but they are relationships of manipulation that do not build healthy connections, professionally or personally. This is a world where more than once I've had people try to throw me under the bus. These types of interactions cost us as people.

We are faced with the same risks when it comes to friends. We need friends we can confide in. It is good not to keep things on our chest. We have to be careful though. I'm still teaching myself how to trust with caution. I've been burned before and no matter what I do, I will be burned again. That is a fact of life.

We should be selective with our inner circles even as we do open ourselves up to trust others. With females in particular, there is a part of us that has that nurturing soul, but there is another side that can gossip and judge. We see it everywhere, even in the church, where it shouldn't be. I share things and fear certain people will judge me for it or they will be quick to tell others my confidences. This is why we should trust, but be careful who we surround ourselves with.

There is a saying that you keep your friends close, but your enemies closer. The idea is that when you know your enemy, you should keep an eye on them in order to keep them within your confidence to know what they are planning. In the end, these pretend friendships with people we consider our enemies are not healthy for anyone. There are too many of these false, political friendships. We hurt each other by behaving in this underhanded way. We destroy trust.

I say keep God closer. God can judge me, but He'll forgive. Spiritually speaking, I do hear Him and feel His presence. We should confide in God first. I try to ask Him to direct me, to show me His will, and to surround me with the right people at the right time. We have to stop fighting God's plans for our lives and stop withholding our trust from God. We must stop wrestling with God and wrestling with trust. It's time to let Him win in our lives and trust that that is for the best.

I've gotten good advice and resources from the right people placed in my life. I appreciate that. I've run into people recently who are writing their own books too. For me, in those moments, these are the right people at the right time. We are going through similar things with similar goals. One woman summed up our finding each other in this moment in our lives as, "Ain't nothing but Jesus." She sent me materials about fighting writer's block. We are the right people for each other's lives at a moment where we can lift each other up and help each other toward our goals.

We have to have the discernment to extinguish too. Some people come into our lives with genuine intentions and they earn our trust. We choose to risk trust upon them. Others come seeming genuine, but they have other motives. Some people operate under hidden envy. They destroy others' lives or they love to have a scoop to share with other people when it is not theirs to tell.

It should be a red flag when a person comes to you with someone else's business and says, "Promise you won't tell. You can't say nothing'." You should tell them, no thank you. They are bringing someone else's confidence to you for a selfish fulfillment for themselves. You can't trust them. They will use that sharing of other people's business with you to get secrets from you to share with others in the same way. This is not the kind of person you need in your life or business.

I have a lady in my life that I consider a true friend. She knows what I'm going through and what I've been through. We have Motivational Mondays together where we call each other up and pray for each other. She's like and angel for me in my life. These are the type of people God sends into our lives.

Seeking God first and trusting Him will open me up to trusting others. I will get hurt from time to time, but it is worth the times that our trust is risked and returned. One day I will find the right man that God wants me to marry. I can trust Him in that. That is not something I have to worry about other than to stop wrestling against God's plan and instead trust Him with control of my life. This is a time where you want to let God win.

Romans 15:13

*May the **God** of hope fill you with all joy and peace as you **trust in** him, so that you may overflow with hope by the power of the Holy Spirit.*

CHAPTER 9: WHAT IF . . .

We question our motives, our moods, and our choices. "What if" is the question we use to come up with excuses, to express our wildest fears of the future, and to try to stop our forward progress? "What if" could be a great phrase that opens us up to new ideas, but most often we use it to shut down.

What if I never get the job I'm looking for?

What if I never get my credit repaired?

What if I never get the house I've dreamed of?

What if I fail?

What if I never get married?

What if I never get to travel to places I haven't seen yet?

What if everyone finds out that I don't know what I am doing?

What if ... What if ... What if ...

"What if" in general guides so many of the choices and non-choices we make in life; those choices shape our whole future.

What if I don't lose the weight?

What if I don't live up to my parents' standards?

What if I fail at being a mother?

"What if" is the language of fear for many of us. We express our insecurities and the weaknesses we see in ourselves. We reveal our lack of control and we are petrified by it.

I imagine I'm not the only one here going through a "What if" phase. Many of you out there are struggling with the same fears, doubts, and barriers.

We wonder about the things that might fall through the cracks. We can't know everything and we can't do it all ourselves. That terrifies us.

So, my question is: *What if it does?*

Let's imagine the plan does come apart or we fail as we all do. Let's get past the "What if" and see exactly "**What is**" on the other side of all those imagined fears. Some of them do come true. Most of what we fear does not actually happen. Something else we never could have expected sneaks up on us and surprises us every time, but for the sake of this discussion, let's say you do see the dreaded "what if" coming and it happens just as you expected. Then what?

"What if" eventually has to be turned back on us. We have to see our part in the problem and we have to see our part in the solution. There needs to be a focus on what we are able to do now to deal with the "what if's" now and for our futures.

We as human beings have to stop questioning life as if it is something outside ourselves that we are just watching and waiting to happen.

We need to commit ourselves to living life to the fullest. Life is what we are and not something that is just happening to us.

I sometimes would regret all the choices that took my life in a different direction away from my dreams and aspirations. Having regrets is not the same thing as living in regrets or dwelling on regrets. Life did not just happen to me. It was my choices then and it is still my choices now. I could say, "What if I had done it all differently, where would I be now?" I can also say, "What if I never achieve some of my goals and I allow fear to hold me back in life?" Neither of these is helpful; if I keep life outside of me and just worry about what will happen to me I will never move forward.

We need to dissect our "what if's" and really understand what is behind them and what we should do about them, if anything. It falls back on ourselves even when there is so much in life that is out of our control. We can only deal with the parts that are in our control. What are we doing with our part? Fate is a concept used to describe the path of our lives and a destiny that is out of our control. We do control parts of our fate. We have free will. God has a purpose for our lives that matches up with the design of our souls, our spirits, and our lives. We control our choices within that design from following our path.

Even when we make mistakes and life seems to be flying out of control, it is still on us to decide what to do next. That may mean seeking help to stop the pattern of mistakes or to get us off a downward spiral. But ultimately, it is our responsibility to seek that help and use that help to its fullest. Whether we involve others or not, it is on us to set a path that leads to the successes we want and need in life.

CHAPTER 10: FORGIVENESS IS RELEASE

This book has been a breakthrough for me spiritually, emotionally, and mentally. I realized part way through that I could not spend my time telling others about struggle, triumph, and redemption without allowing a transformation within myself.

It was a true test. Just like with everything else in my life, I felt the definite calling to do this; I was given the vision, God provided me all the resources I needed, and I constantly fought the urge to just quit and let it go. This book and the process of reexamining my life have taught me some hard truths about myself and seeing this through was part of my own transformation.

If I discovered that my voice was my purpose, I had to do the work to be sure I did not stop in the middle of a sentence. I know now that part of what I am supposed to do with my voice is to give and seek forgiveness.

Few acts in life carry the same healing power of forgiveness. Forgiveness gives all of Christianity its meaning. It gives new meaning to life as well. It heals others and it heals ourselves. A life without forgiveness is a life full of poison.

I thought about and struggled with this topic early on in the writing. When it really hit me hard was on Friday the thirteenth, before the Sunday of Father's Day. My dad lost his job. That is such a simple phrase that everyone understands. We all get how that lands for people, but there is some depth to this that you have to understand to get how deeply this cut for my father.

After my dad left the military, he went right to work for a printing company. It was the only job he really ever had and he held it for the last forty-five years. The banks took over after the company's bankruptcy and they cut him loose. They cut away everything – the paycheck, the pension, the built up vacation days, everything.

All of this right before Father's Day. He told me, "I'm really going to feel this for the first time on Monday."

Forty-five years of Mondays he has gone into that job. He doesn't know how to write a resume. Why would he need to know how? That job was something we all just took for granted.

My father worked hard all his life. He was taught that that was what it took and he taught that to all of us through his words and deeds. He could make a dollar out of fifteen cents. I used to call him cheap. He had three-hundred hours of vacation built up unused that are just gone.

We live in a small town with limited opportunities for a man of any age - much less a man of sixty-two years with no other experience in any field. You always need a plan B because even the safe life can fall out from under you at any moment.

I tell you all that to say this. There is not much in life we can afford to take for granted. That includes family, friends, jobs, our life, and tomorrow. This fact makes forgiveness, especially among family, all the more important.

I have two older siblings: a brother that is seven years older and a sister that is four years older. I'm going to try to explain this in the least complicated way possible. My brother and I have the same mom, but different biological fathers. My sister and I have the same father, but different mothers and we grew up in different houses less than a mile apart. Though my brother and I grew up in the same home and the same family, it was a different home and a different family for each of us. My parents were together and my family was whole. It was a different type of blended family for my brother and that much more so for my sister too.

My brother and I were close growing up despite the age difference. He left for the army and served in the Gulf War in the early nineties. After the army, he went on with his life and I felt like I'd lost my best friend. He and I didn't really connect again after he left.

He got a good job and was able to help provide for the family financially. He could buy nice gifts for my parents at Christmas and give back to them in ways I couldn't with everything I was putting myself through.

It wasn't competition, but it felt like one the way many things between siblings do. I was a single mom and I felt like I was looked at differently by the family. My parents had to give to me, while my brother could give to them. I wanted to be able to do that someday, but he did it.

Ten years ago, I tried to reconnect with my brother and he let out some feelings I wasn't expecting. He told me that I had it made while he had to work for everything. My brother had to fend for himself. As my parents looked after me, he had to get rides home from games and walk home sometimes. He had to get a job to get his own car. He did not have the same relationship with my dad that I did. He told me I was spoiled. That was hard to hear and whether it was true or not, I was not in a place to hear it at the time.

My dad was not an outwardly emotional man. Our home was not abusive, but there was bickering between us – the siblings especially. My mom told me once that our family had a generational curse. With all that the parents and children in our family go through and put each other through generation after generation, we are sometimes about the business of passing down pain. We could have our own reality show. I had the same conversation with my sister.

She and I had the same father, but grew up in different houses. I did not know about her through a good part of my growing up even though she lived just half a mile away. She knew about me. Every birthday she watched my father drive past her house to go to his other family up the street. He did see her, but he lived at our house and that's not the same.

Going into the ninth grade in high school, I knew at that point that she was a senior. I could not go to her for advice or seek her out for help. It was a strange situation.

She told me that I got the whole family, the house, the holidays, the fence, the dog, and everything. After these conversations, I felt like I was being attacked by my brother and sister. I was just a kid growing up, and I didn't ask for it. As I grew older, I saw what they meant. I could look back through their eyes and understand a little better.

After I got myself out of living in my car out by the beach, I did not come back to live at home. I moved to Virginia in the Northern D.C. area to start a new life for me and my daughter.

I distanced myself on purpose. It wasn't that I thought I was better. It was that home was the one horse town everyone talks about with no room for growth for me. It was the kind of town where you could work the same job for forty-five years and have it dry up on you. If I had stayed there or returned there, I would probably be a single mom with multiple kids, dependent on the system, and probably on all the substances that I nearly did not escape. I look at my cousins who stayed and what they do that they've always done. Every time I am back there, I see the people that never left and seem to have never changed either. Going home is draining for me.

My family knows if they want see me more than twice a year, they have to come out to see me. I don't want to feel like home is only for Christmas and Mother's Day. I don't like going through the motions with family to try to be cordial for the sake of our mother. I want family to be more than holidays and death.

Pride gets in the way. It takes someone being the bigger person. We can spend our whole lives looking around and waiting for others to play that part for us. Many families do.

I've had several folks tell me, "You have to be the root to your family."

I am in the center in a way. I'm not perfect, and I'm not the most deserving. I am in a way the connection between my siblings, parents, and other points of my family. I did not ask to be born there, but they do have the connection to each other through me. I need to stop looking around for someone else to be the bigger person.

We have layers of hurt between us swollen with pride. When I lay in bed at night and can't find it in me to forgive or let go of the anger, I'm giving power to the hurt and negativity. I'm feeding it in my life. We give power to those that hurt us even though they are not there with us and have no idea what we are even thinking or feeling in that moment.

The Lord's direction is so clear. I can't let people or situations steal the happiness of my family any longer. I can't do it anymore. I want to make things right and finally give back.

When we go about forgiving others, we often add on, "but I can't forget." It is true in one very real sense, but that can also be a new kind of poison we drink that kills the forgiveness, withers our happiness, and eventually kills our own soul.

Forgiveness, truly open forgiveness, aligns us in the right direction and sets us free in a way that most things can not. It releases our heart and mind. If we hold on to any piece of the pain, even from someone that does not deserve to be forgiven, we carry that with us and pass it on to the next loved one down the line that had no part in making that pain. Without forgiving and letting go of the ones that abused me, I doom my future relationships for what a previous boyfriend has done. I add to the generational curse that does not come from magic, but from our own unforgiving hearts.

By the time this book ends and it sits in your hands, I want to have made amends with my siblings. I want to be in the kind of peace that only comes from true forgiveness. We won't just get along because that's what our mother wants from the kids.

All relationships, from the most healthy to the most destructive, demand forgiveness. Do not stay in bad relationships full of abuse, but don't carry that pain in your heart all your life either. Do not keep it on you like a curse you can't shake. Many of us carry pain from our past from people that died years ago. When we decide to forgive, it is not just about releasing that other person, dead or alive, from responsibility for what they did or said. It is more about releasing ourselves from a life sentence of pain that we are enforcing on ourselves all alone. Forgiveness is about setting ourselves free and in that process we release more pain. Everyone around us will experience healing, including our poor loved ones that don't even know why they are suffering.

There will always be people in our lives that we must put out of our lives, forgiven or not. There are others that are out of our lives even when they are right next to us because we will not forgive. They deserve to be let back in with love.

Holding onto resentment is a full-time job that we work hard at year after year for decades. It is a dead end job that pays only in pain and does not let us use any vacation days. We work at it and work at it until we don't even consider doing anything else. Then, one day, the people we couldn't forgive are gone and we truly suffer the pain all alone. The job of being unforgiving is done and can never be taken back to heal that relationship.

Don't do that to yourself. Free your heart and mind by forgiving. Rebuild relationships on peace, without all the baggage we shouldn't be carrying anyway. The curse may be ours to carry, and but it is also ours to lift.

Don't take anything for granted, especially the idea that we might have time to forgive and rebuild tomorrow.

Let's resolve together to forgive them and rebuild the relationships worthy of rebuilding, starting with the ones closest to us.

CHAPTER 11: IT DOESN'T HAVE TO BE YOUR DESTINY

My maternal grandmother is almost eighty years old. She lives in the same town near and around my family where I grew up. I don't come home often, and when I do, I'm ready to leave.

It was on my heart to call my grandmother the other day. At first, she confused me for one of my cousins. It took a while, but once she finally figured out who I was, she acted happy to hear from me. She was surprised to hear from me and it seemed to make her day.

I could hear something else in her voice too. Laced in with the confusion was the sound of a woman who had been drinking. I think it is a foregone conclusion that my grandmother is an alcoholic. She's stopped going to church and is seen as the neighborhood drunk going around looking for work and money to get more to drink.

I want to help her, but I'm not sure exactly how. Even as I went through all my struggles, seeing her now is a warning of where I could have ended up; but, by the grace of God, I did not.

If she were to leave today, I would remember her as a good grandmother. She was working nine to five and taking care of the kids. She took an active role in my life, telling me on a constant basis that I could be someone. Someone just meeting her now would not see that person that I remember.

I could trace for you what changed for her from then to now and I will, but that is not her whole story. And this is where my mother's notion of our family's generational curse comes from in large part.

When my mother was young, my grandmother was like she is now. This is the childhood my mother remembers and holds in her heart. My mom was eight and had to dress herself because my grandmother was nowhere to be found or least not home. She walked to the bus stop all mismatched and teased by the other kids. Then, her mother, my grandmother, went stumbling along for everyone to see in her nightgown from another house on her way home.

My mother ended up pregnant with my brother when she was a young teen by an older man. Today, that would be seen as statutory rape. For my mom, it was just life and the family generational curse. Where I come from a lot of things you just hid under the rug and kept it moving.

My grandmother got it together and became the kind, church-going woman I remember, but my mother never forgot what was taken from her that early in her life because of this woman's behavior and problems. When my grandmother went back to that life and those problems, all that old resentment reawakened in my mother's heart.

My grandmother lost her daughter, my aunt, in the shooting I described earlier. We ignored the signs of what grandmother was going through with that loss because we were all dealing with it too.

We mourned, got over it, and moved on. Even her kids dealt with it in their own ways. Now it is obvious looking back that grandmother wasn't dealing with it, getting over it, or getting past it. We didn't know what she was feeling. As years went by, we healed and moved on as she spiraled down.

We did what we do as a family in feeding our own curses. We ignored the obvious. She had her own place, and it was easy to put her aside as we dealt with our own lives and our own issues.

In terms of this generational curse, I have other family members I knew as a kid that are just gone. They got strung out on drugs or some sort of addiction and were not tolerated by our family. My favorite uncle as a kid went through this and ended up moving to another state never to be heard from again until years later. That's how stuff around here gets handled, and it isn't helping any of us.

I need to have this talk with my mother.

From 2000 or 2001 until now, the family gradually distanced themselves from grandmother. People don't visit her now. She mentioned it in her phone conversation with me. Her twin sister doesn't come by, her son doesn't call, the local family in town doesn't spend time with her, and I'm no different trying to get out of town as quickly as I arrive.

I could hear the alcohol in her voice. I recognized the familiar tones. It's not fair of me, but this gave me mixed emotions. Hearing it all got me angry, but also confused and sad. She is the older generation and is supposed to have it all together.

She went from passably good to worse a few years ago. That's when she fell off her porch because she was drunk. She got a serious bruise on her head, but was lucky she didn't end up dead. Being in the hospital, she was away from alcohol for a while. As my mother brought her home after just twenty-four hours, with instructions to watch for the signs of concussion, my grandmother already had a serious case of the shakes from withdrawal.

My mother asked, "Do you want me to stop and get you a beer?"

My grandmother said, "Yeah, if you don't mind."

My mother stopped at a gas station and went in to buy a can of beer. She is a proper church woman and knew nothing about the process of getting a can of beer. She figured it out and got back to the car where my grandmother gulped it down, putting down the shakes enough to get it together. My mother watched it and couldn't bear it.

Grandmother went from a Christian lady to a grumpy, old, complaining alcoholic. No one wants to be around her. Family gatherings went from her house to my mom's house.

I never reached that point, but I can relate to her and what she is going through to some extent. When people go through something like divorce or death or anything else life shattering, they react differently. Depression and anxiety set in for some and they look to cope. Some want to mask what they are dealing with. I heard pain in her voice and I tried to tell her I understood. I knew the feeling of being an outsider, even if I couldn't fully comprehend her loss. I'm not sure I got through.

I don't want to be like her - and she reminds me so much of myself. I don't want to get old and grumpy and be written off by the family like she has been. I want to leave some kind of meaningful legacy. Seeing the family judging her and what she is going through is very personal to me.

As a family unit, we never took the time. We didn't get her the help. One of my cousins questioned why the woman couldn't just let go. In the South and in the African American community, seeking help with emotional and mental issues is a taboo. Back in the day, it was seen as weakness and meant you were crazy. People have to get past this for themselves and members of their families. People have to seek the help they need with loss, pain, and addiction. . In Acts 20:35, we are reminded "In everything I did, I showed you that by this kind of hard work we must *help* the weak, remembering the words the Lord Jesus himself said: 'It is more blessed to give than to receive.' "

What's very telling about my grandmother's state now is that it has gotten to the point that my mom and uncle have had to step in to handle her finances and affairs.

We have to acknowledge and accept. We don't have to approve or excuse, but maintaining her or anyone else we love in a state of self-destruction is no way for anyone or their family to live. We can look down on folks for being addicted to something, in a dysfunctional relationship, or on the system, but it does not raise us or them. Regardless of their flaws or failures, forgiveness and acceptance go further to healing and lifting than judgment ever could

This is why I have been so secretive about my struggles. I don't share and haven't shared in the past because I don't want to be a target of that judgment. To this day, I don't want to experience my mother's judgment. As an adult, I hide things partially out of a sense of respect, not wanting my mother to know my failings that would feed her pained notion of the generational curse. But does my "respectful" secrecy actually serve her or the family? With my flaws, I don't want to be judged. I want to be embraced and helped.

Be there for that person. This does not mean to sink into their addictions with them or to stay with someone when you are mutually self-destructive, but when someone you love is down and you are in a position to reach, then reach.

We have to come together for one, real intervention on her behalf. This act is not just for her, but it is a necessary family act to break the generational curse we have all just accepted as reality. We can't just be satisfied to say nice things about her at her funeral. I don't want to end up like that and I don't want to leave the family in a state to allow it. I want to be part of the mending.

My mother's reaction to what little she has known about my mistakes in the past is to say, "Tressa, you just acting crazy right now."

But addiction must be faced to be solved, just like most problems in life, but more so with issues of addiction. Addiction doesn't have a color, religion, or creed. It is bipartisan and holds no prejudice. Addiction is there for every type of victim and every type of family. It is very real when you are going through it. You ain't "just acting crazy". You have a problem that needs to be faced whether you are the one with the addiction or the one who loves the person struggling with it.

My God has told me to give my all. If I'm holding back, I'm not fulfilling that call. I say it again: I want to be part of the mending. This does not have to be destiny. For the one struggling with addiction or the ones struggling and suffering alongside that person, this does not have to be a set destiny. This is not the last chapter of your lives. It does not have to be.

So, what can we do now?

Mending our relationships is a worthy pursuit. We like to say we are independent and don't need family, but we want someone real to share our good times with. We all have flaws and have done something. Dysfunction is always hidden on the inside and underneath. Sometimes we like being around other families more than our own because their issues can remain hidden from us. Don't give into your family's generational curse. Breaking the cycles and facing the problems will help everyone involved. Seeking help yourself and guiding others you love to seek it out is a worthy goal. You may be satisfied for now to hide these things to avoid judgment and confrontation, but there is very little satisfaction in waiting to say something nice at a funeral. Act now while healing and meaningful forgiveness are still possible.

CHAPTER 12: NEVER SETTLE FOR THE BARE MINIMUM

I wish I could say never settle for the bare minimum in life, but we are all way past that point. I can say don't settle for the bare minimum any longer.

We get into survival mode and don't try for anything higher. We set our sights on the just taking the next step, which is the best we can do at some points in life, but then stop on that step.

This is not a life of purpose, and it has to change.

In our jobs, relationships, and other situations, we settle for just being where we are and we don't try for anything more.

Why do we do that?

Sometimes we do it to be there for our kids as best we can. Sometimes we settle for the bare minimum because of financial concerns. Other times we use age as an excuse not to try for anything more.

These things keep us from stepping out of our comfort zone. We will either leap on faith, or we just leap without any belief or notion of where or why. Progress can only come in that leap of faith.

Without that faith, we don't go after our dreams at all or we go after them with a limited timeframe in mind. We are willing to pursue for a while, but then we are ready to hit the kill switch and go back to living the bare minimum life all over again. That bottom rung is always there waiting for us when we are ready to rest and give up on climbing.

This goes back to relationships for many of us. We stick with someone that is not good for us and helps set the low bar on life for us. Women in particular are willing to stick with the guy that is no good, but is there. We think we couldn't possibly leave. If we did, we think we are not pretty enough, we are overweight, and no one else would want us. The idea that the right significant other is out there is another dream we are not willing to pursue, so we hit the kill switch on that idea before we even start. The idea that we might be okay pursuing the next phase in life alone for a while is terrifying to many of us. Just like with many other aspects of our lives, we become complacent and we stay.

We give up before we start.

I had a child at an early age. I graduated pregnant. While my peers were going off to college, I scratched that notion off my dream list. I needed to provide a life for my daughter and I wasn't willing to consider other dreams to be a part of that. I decided I had to settle for the father and make the best of the life I had created for myself on the bottom rung.

High school love has that funny, intense quality of feeling like everything, but sometimes really being nothing at all. Some people follow that high school sweetheart and they develop into real, mature love over a lifetime. Most are better off by moving on, learning from young mistakes, and building lasting relationships as they become older and wiser. Having a daughter that young had forever tied me to my high school sweetheart and made him a part of my history. That would prove to be a painful and dangerous part of my life.

I do believe I am more than those circumstances earlier in my life that shaped the hard edges of my path through those years. God has put creative ideas in my head that I am finally beginning to act upon. I do believe He has put extraordinary potential in me and my life, and I am finally starting to allow that potential to become action and reality. I may have settled in my younger years, but I'm changing that now and I believe you can too.

I am not ordinary. I refuse to be. I refuse to act like I am just ordinary and I refuse to be pushed down until ordinary is all I ever accomplish in this life. I'm done with that. I will not settle for the bare minimum from myself or for myself – not anymore. I have the God given capacity to be extraordinary.

God has given me the resources to be more. He gives me the pieces I need to execute the actions to meet my purpose and I will not be that ordinary person that used to give up so quickly when trouble came or the path got difficult.

I'm done holding back on what I want to say. I'm through settling for the minimum from my voice and calling it careful. I still have the little girl with dreams inside me. She is still crying for help. She is the core of me underneath the woman with a voice waiting to finally say what I have meant to say for so long.

Women in particular are conditioned to settle by so much of the structure and circumstance of life. We are dealing with being the housewives, coming to grips with what it means to be divorced, or finding ourselves offered the supporting role by life. Whatever our circumstances, our purpose is going to demand of us that we fully utilize our talents.

My first piece of advice to women in this regard is to build the right circle of friends to nurture your talent and potential. Women can be awful to themselves and each other. Getting the right folks in your life to help you get a leg up is no easy task, but it may be a vital step to helping you finally rise toward your purpose.

Earlier, I talked about how my father lost the job that defined his life. He was understandably complacent after so many decades at the same job. When it was snatched from him, it was as if they were trying to steal a piece of his identity. In his complacency on the same rung of the ladder where he had always felt safe and comfortable, he could have been bettering himself in the unforeseen event that the job he took for granted might be gone one day. He didn't know this and he did not make a plan B.

As a contractor, I could see when our company was not winning new work. I too could stay put, hold on, and hope for the best. Those don't sound like a bad idea from the outside. But, it is not a plan B and that behavior doesn't always move us along with our purpose in life. Employers in this type of work react to hard times by cutting staff and reducing hours. Facing this reality means being proactive and looking at what might be next in life instead of waiting to be thrown out.

It means looking for the hope to be found at the end of the rope. For many of us it means more school or even free classes where they might be offered to build new skills; but, it **does not** mean feeling stuck or hopeless.

Life does not have to be a picnic for us to succeed. Often, we find the opposite to be true as we struggle toward the successes in life that really matter. If we find ourselves buried in a life of unhappiness though, it often defeats our journey toward our purpose.

I'm reawakening a business that I've been keeping on the backburner from my days of giving up too easily. I kept the domain name and had all the setup in place. Even though I had not followed through before, I still had the pieces in place, just waiting for me to have the guts to make a real try again.

Even as I rebrand my own approach to life, I began to rebrand the business ideas I started, but had not yet seen through. I have developed important corporate skills, and I'm ready to bring those skills together with my greater purpose.

I had a friend tell me. "I've heard this all before, but it never happens. Just do it. If you're going to do it this time, then just do it."

That stung a little. I know the truth about where I have failed before. I know better than anyone, except for God himself, about that aspect of my life. I was looking for validation and that is a big piece of my mistake in really finding and engaging my purpose. I always want someone to tell me it is a good idea. I was missing that for so long on so many things. I want to do it right this time, which means doing it a little differently. I've always wanted to blurt out what I was thinking of doing and have the validation for it come from others on the outside. When I didn't find that, and usually I didn't, I immediately wanted to change my mindset back to survival, complacency, and settling for the minimum.

True validation can't come from others that happen to be around you at the moment. If for no other reason, it can't come from some of them because they might be the exact people sitting on the bottom rung with you refusing to climb. They don't want you climbing up and leaving them behind. They might be happy for you to stay down low with them waiting for that safe piece of ladder to snap right out from under you.

No, today has to be different. I can't allow others to decide to validate what God is leading me to do. I have to resolve within myself to rise up to meet the purpose being revealed to me. My other choice is to stay stuck and that is never our purpose.

This time I'm taking the time and following through to see that A aligns to B which leads to C and so forth. I'm not spinning out of control this time to end up in a bind that gives me the excuse to give up all over again.

Going after a creative idea is still work. It requires time and commitment. It demands vision being translated into purposeful action. It requires faith and a steadfast spirit.

With all that in mind, I warn you again to be cautious who you share ideas and dreams with, especially in the early stages. When we are scared, we are easier to defeat. Our dreams are not for everyone and not everyone can handle them - nor should everyone be trusted with something as precious as our dreams. This goes back to finding the right circle to help us move upward. A person with all cons or even all pros is not going to be the best help in meeting our purpose or reaching our dreams. People outside the world you are entering will not be able to fully understand it or give meaningful insight into facing it. They are of a different mindset. A good circle needs to include new people within the new world that understand the pitfalls, the celebrations, and the struggles of that world. Your circle also needs trusted allies who support you and can give you perspective from the outside as well. You are building a team as you dream.

There is a principle from the Bible of not letting your left hand know what your right hand is doing. The primary interpretation and context of that idea is being humble and not boasting on our good deeds taking the glory away from God. I do think there is a deeper, more subtle warning in that too. Sharing the work and business of one hand with another that is engaged in different, unrelated work may not help either accomplish their tasks. While both the left and right hand can work together and often must to accomplish a task, I believe this Biblical passage speaks to the fact that sometimes a task is meant for one and not the other. Trying to write with the wrong hand feels like an alien activity and produces poor work. If you type with proper technique, but cross your hands to opposite sides of the keyboard from where they belong, you will end up with an unintelligible mess. If both hands try to turn on a light, unscrew a cap on a bottle, or other such simple tasks not meant to involve both hands, something simple becomes disastrous.

Likewise, there are people in my life I would not want to lose anymore than I would want to lose my right or left hand. This idea means though that they may not be meant to be involved in everything I'm involved in. Our purposes in life may not match. Adding me to their pursuits or adding them to my dreams and purpose may be destructive to both of us. There may be things we are meant to do together, but there are others where not everyone is meant to take part. Select your circle well when it comes to your calling and purpose.

Another simple suggestion I would make would be to jot down your ideas. It may not be time to plant or harvest yet and an important idea may need time to develop and season. It may be a seed that needs to be planted during a different season of your life. By writing it, we give it a name and substance. We can meditate on it and understand its place in our purpose better. This is not say that we excuse ourselves for hesitating or procrastinating. At the same time, we don't blunder forward with no thought or consideration. Every great act involves some leap of faith. These leaps are often to places we can't see before we have jumped which is why so many people never take the necessary leap. Still, blundering is not the same as leaping. When the time does come, we must leap boldly out of our comfort zone and into our purpose with faith.

All the inner demons will try to cut you down the entire journey, but especially at the beginning. The baggage we carry can drag us down and hinder our progress, if not stop it completely. Holding on to envy, hatred, or impatience can kill our dreams as completely as the worst people in our lives. Getting rid of the dream killers in our lives also means getting rid of the feelings we hold on to and blame on those people that have hurt us. Growth in life is often painful and often means growing out of these negative feelings we harbor even if we feel they are justified feelings. Hate and envy are not good conditions for growth. They do not connect to purpose. They lead to a minimal life and we don't have to live that way anymore.

People that have lost jobs or have been hurt will find depression very easily. They just want to give up. They want to end their journey in one fashion or another. Even if that just means settling for the minimum in life, it is not what we are meant to do. It is not what we are meant to be.

This is a new season for my life. I have to wake up with a purpose. Most successful people do just that. I think I'm successful and I believe I am meant to be. A life of faith and a mindset toward success are tools I am choosing to give myself as I use my voice and rise to my purpose. We do not have to settle for the minimum in life anymore.

Galatians 6:9

Let us not become weary in doing good, for at the proper time we will reap a harvest if *we do not give up*.

CHAPTER 13: HEALTH MATTERS

I've tried to lose weight many times. I have failed as often as anyone out there. It is a familiar story because it is a familiar struggle. I've always started well. It is finishing badly that is my problem. Looking back, I believe I have started at least ten different diet systems. With all of them, I struggle to finish.

This last time, I woke up on a Monday morning and looked in a mirror as I often do. I was at an all-time high on weight, creeping up to almost 190. Yikes! Each time we reach a new all-time high, it's a new milestone until the next time. I was ready for a change. I can't expect results if there is no change. So, what makes this time different from all the other times? The truth is not much, if the result ends up being the same, but this is more than just about weight. When I look in the mirror with dissatisfaction, it is about more than physical appearance. When I want to live a healthier life, it is a decision I'm making that has more involved than eating healthy. In this life change, I want to live healthier emotionally and spiritually as well. That is different than any of the numerous times before.

It took me years to put on weight; it will take time to take it off. It took me years to pile on all my emotional baggage. There will be a process in shedding both types of weight. But enough is enough.

I searched out a weight loss center in my area. I had gone through all the crash diets myself. I had bought into the promises of late night infomercials in the past. I'd failed at many do-it-yourself plans. I was looking to get some skin in the game and have myself held accountable.

I was still skeptical though. I went in for my health screening. I had an EKG, bloodwork, etc. There were some abnormalities on the EKG that obviously concerned me. I'm following up with my doctor, but in the meantime, that is just a reminder that I need to live in healthier ways now.

Something made me commit to the program this time. I've put money into gyms I rarely visited. I dumped money into protein shakes and the diet program foods before without finishing out. This time I was looking for something more.

The first major adjustment for me this time is that I needed to cut sugar and alcohol. The shock to my lifestyle on these told me more about myself than just my problems with weight. This addressed my methods of coping and my choices for comfort. Cutting these things from my life would help my body shed pounds, but I was shedding other baggage as well. I had to detox myself and my life. Habits and consequences of habits were being extracted from my life and body.

I was less than three years away from forty at the time that I wrote this. There are changes that happen to us physically, but also in maturity. We can fight and deny those things or we can embrace them and use those opportunities to grow in a way that we were meant to long ago. If I allow my body and my life to become healthy through these changes, I will reach a point where I am no longer fighting to regain ground, but just working to maintain my gains. That is a goal worth pursuing in many areas of our lives.

I have fed my body unhealthy garbage and I have filled my life with unhealthy situations at many points along the way. Cutting alcohol from my life for weight loss reasons is good for me, but doing so now instead of later is vital to me for my quality of life in coming years and decades.

Getting the questionable result on the EKG concerned me for my heart. I knew about my stress and anxiety. I knew it had physical symptoms. This wake up call about my weight has led to a wake up call for my health which is directly connected to a wake up call for every aspect of my life.

Being on a new diet tends to make me cranky at first. This time was no different in that regard. I took the initiative to declutter my cabinets. I was removing temptation, but also streamlining my life and lifestyle. Leaving old pieces that have no place in your new path is just more weight and burden on a process that is already difficult. Throwing those things out is a part of the shedding process.

I went to the store to buy replacement items that were fresh and healthy. As many of us discover, unhealthy comes cheap these days. It costs greatly in the long run, but bad choices are on sale up front. Quality costs. This is true in groceries, but it is true in all life changes too. There is a sacrifice in doing what is right. Always.

I got groceries that were good for me. I wrote down what I ate and drank more water. I could feel the difference and the challenge to stick with it as my body began the process of running off stored fat. Unfortunately, as we all know, adding on fat cells is a much faster process than trying to burn off fat. There is a price that is paid in the choices that get us here, so the process of improving deals with those choices and their consequences. There's nothing to do about it, except to stick with it.

On the other side of these initial struggles, my energy levels have picked up. I even went to the gym from the motivation of that extra energy. I gained more energy from that choice and that small victory. As with all things, those that are holding me accountable reminded me that if I stick with it, I will see results.

A side effect of this is that things seem much clearer to me. Being healthy in my life choices has had an effect on my stress. I'm not groggy or tired. There is a reach to both our good choices and our bad choices that extend out into other areas of our lives. Making an improvement in one area can have a net effect elsewhere.

So, don't be afraid to get rid of the unhealthy in your life. This includes the physical, but also spiritual, emotional, and relational. Bad relationships, romantic or otherwise, can drag down every part of our lives. Be healthy in all our choices in all these areas. Shed the old pieces of life that add weight to the process of living a better life.

I was tested by a Happy Hour at work recently. There would be alcohol and fried appetizers. I declined because I knew myself. I'd just have a little to start with, but then ... but then. Maybe someday soon, I'll be able to go for the fellowship while still being true to my own choices, but that's not now. I was proud of myself.

You can do anything with the right mindset. In the past, I wanted a quick fix. I wanted to have my cake and eat it too. I tried to cheat the process.

Accountability is helpful. Sometimes it's vital. I check in. In this case, I get weighed, take pictures, etc. Accountability works in changing other life habits. It helps with the spiritual too. It is based on trust and honesty. You have to open yourself up to both in an accountability relationship.

As people, we need an extra push. It is easy for me to slip up. I'm good at slipping up. I don't want to see my efforts go to waste though. I might reach a point where I'm past some of these desires and they don't have the same hold on my life that they had in the past. For now, I stay focused and accountable for my choices.

I extend these better life choices into my financial decisions and friendship decisions. All of these choices touch on the healthy choices we do or don't make in our lives. If these choices are not helping us grow personally or professionally, a change needs to be made. People come into our lives for a reason and sometimes for a season. Not everyone stays and sometimes it is time for certain relationships to go for the good of everyone involved.

Assess where you are in life. What doesn't make sense for you anymore? What is hurting you? Who brings positivity? Who is a bastion of bad news?

I had a habit at one point in my life of spending ten or twenty dollars a day on the lottery. That money could go toward paying down bills or saving for a house. I stopped having cash on me when I went to the gas station. In my financial life, that lottery habit was my unhealthy snacking and it had to be let go.

We need to detox these things from our lives. It's never too late. Don't put off until tomorrow what you can do today because it will not be easier tomorrow. Our cheat days become quitting. We start our diets in life at the beginning of the week or after the holidays. Promises become broken promises. New Year's resolutions become February failures. Start today because today is in your power. Waiting is often planning for failure.

We control what we take into our bodies and our lives. By doing this, we can eventually control what we desire. A support system, accountability, and detoxing bad habits from your system are good for any change in your life. Healthier choices have a sweeping effect over every part of our lives. This is so much bigger than just weight. This is about making the choices for a quality life and paying the costs for that quality. If I can do it, others can too. You will have an opportunity join me on this journey in my second book.

CHAPTER 14: LOVE AND OUR TIMELINE

This is a sensitive topic for single women in particular. Part of the difficulty in discussing this is that we've all heard it in one form or another. *You don't need a man to make you happy. Mr. Right will come along in time. You have to be patient. You are being too picky or you are not picky enough. A good man is hard to find. When the time is right ...* and so on. It gets to just be noise and this same list of clichés is thrown at single men in other forms. When a person is in the midst of struggling with the ideas of love, relationships, and "the one," these lines of advice don't seem to help much.

Another part of the difficulty with this topic is that our egos are wrapped up in the vision of what an ultimate committed relationship is supposed to be, when it is supposed to happen, and what that says about our value as a person.

I've had my share of relationships. I've dated. Sometimes it has gotten serious. Occasionally I have thought they were going places. These didn't last or they didn't go where I wanted.

I would pray and ask God why and list specific things I wanted because we are taught to be specific in our requests. Often, I specifically ask for the wrong things for my life and God knows better than to give me what I don't need. Still, I wanted something different than what I was getting.

We want it all – career woman, soul mate, kids, the American Dream with all its status symbols. Reality sets in as we make choices that bring us closer to some of these things and take us further from others. Today's world sets us up to want it all, but does not equip us to handle everything we get. We juggle a little bit of everything in our lives and end up dropping as much or more than what we catch.

We put ourselves into a set of deadlines based on age.

By 25, I wanted to check off certain things in my life. I wanted my degree. I wanted to be on the beginning of my career path. I wanted a particular direction for my life. More than some other things, I expected to be ready to find love and my soul mate.

I didn't go to college right off because I was pregnant my senior year. That goal and many surrounding it got derailed along with most of my plans.

Being in a relationship from high school and sticking with it beyond then, is a tricky business. Some people find their soul mate then and they make it work for the rest of their lives. Most people do not. It is even more complicated when that relationship is held together by an unexpected pregnancy.

My grandmother always said, "No one is *just* in love in high school. They are <u>dumb</u> *and* in love." When you are young and inexperienced, you can't seem to have one without the other sometimes. Some of us fall hard, dumb, and in love every time, and our decisions reflect that. When you are making life decisions while young, dumb, and in love, you can be in for a hard road filled with a level of consequences you can't possibly understand in the moment. This is the perfect time in life to misidentify "the one." When you get it wrong once, it gets far easier to identify the wrong person as a "soul mate" over and over, adding pain onto pain and hurting our hearts and spirits in the process.

You should not be trying too hard to find this person too early for this very reason. It may come early for some people, but not most people. This arrival of "the one" does not follow our timelines in this way. We have to open to God's time.

At any age, we can be guilty of settling. Being realistic is important. Going for less though is not of value for your life. There is a great deal lost in deciding it is okay to attach your life to a mismatch. You can be unevenly yoked on career goals, beliefs, character, values, and other important life aspects. Each mismatch comes with a price to the value of your life while in that relationship. You do not have to be identical to your match by any means, but there are certain core values that must align or that relationship will never be anything but forced.

By 30, my timeline becomes a little more desperate. Hitting thirty was a bit of a culture shock. My goals from age twenty-five were largely not accomplished. Having a man in my life that could possibly be the one hadn't happened. The full level of success I wanted had not been achieved.

This was a time to re-evaluate for me in a big way. I questioned myself as a person for not being where the age thirty point on my timeline was supposed to be plotted. Particularly, single people at thirty question themselves on what it means about them as a person to still be single. The timeline is getting tight on that plan for our lives.

Again, I approached God and reminded Him that he knew what I wanted and I was specific - as if He did not already know. I still believed that finding a man that was equally spiritually yoked was worth the time and the sacrifice. With my history, I'd prefer someone who had not been married before or who had that part of their life well settled without bringing tons of drama into my and my daughter's lives. With my daughter, I also needed to find a man that had a "sense of fatherhood" in him, which is not every man out there.

Single mothers have added challenges in their quest for love. For a person who has kids, going out with a person that doesn't, it is like crossing between different worlds. The journey is not impossible, but not every person is up for it, and not every couple can make it work.

I think of my parents on this particular point. My brother and father struggled with that very thing. From my brother to me, my father adjusted to the connections, but my brother missed out on some of that. I see the difference in our experiences as we grew up and that is a lot to ask of a child.

You want someone to treat your child like his or her own. Those types of soul mate candidates are hard to find.

This is true of any child, but I think it is especially tough with a female child. There is a lot of emotional and mental harm that can be done by bringing men in and out of a daughter's life. You have to set an example of how she deserves to be treated and what is acceptable. Rotating men through, even if it is just innocent, casual dating, sends a message that she can be taken up and set aside. You must be more cautious with a daughter's life than that.

I did not want my daughter to get attached just to be disappointed when things didn't work out. After three months, six months, or nine months, if it didn't work out, I did not have to explain it over and over. I took the same approach to dating with the rest of my family too. If I wasn't bringing every guy around, I didn't have to explain every break up. I also did not have to explain each new start of the next relationship. Trying to maintain a relationship was challenge enough without the extra eyes and judgment.

I had a friend tell me, "You make time for what you want to make time for."

This is essentially true in dating, too, and priorities in my life have put other things ahead of my dating life very often.

So, I kept my dating life in a bubble. When things lasted over a year and it looked like it might be more serious, I considered letting them in a little more to that part of my life. This may seem strict, but there are parts of my life that deserved great care.

My daughter actually told me, "I don't see you ever getting married."

I was a little taken aback and pressed her as to why.

She told me, "You are too independent. You like your space."

She sees me for who I really am, I suppose. I have worked very hard to develop independence. Being a single mother, you develop a "by any means" attitude toward survival. No matter what happens with jobs, with bills, or with our home, I have to make sure that we make it – my daughter and me. I'm going to hold it down. That translates to independence, I guess.

My daughter has known that I was dating, but she was rarely exposed to any of the men unless I was in a serious relationship. The majority of her friends were from two parent homes. She saw them get things that she couldn't have. She understood that we weren't going to have all that and as she has gotten older, she appreciates more what we worked for together. She understands more now that she is older and getting ready to strike out on her own.

I especially did not want her to ever get the impression that she had to have a man to survive or take care of her. I want her to find love and a complete life, but I don't want her settling for any guy because she sees that as essential. I believe she has learned the skills and strength to take care of herself.

Once she or I end up in the right relationship, I want to know that we are able to bring something to the table and not just to be dependent. If tragedy strikes or hard times, I want the skills to be able to support a family while my partner gets back on his feet.

I've always been big on paying every once and a while. Some men and women don't go for that, but I've never been big on giving the impression that I had to be supported, or that was what the relationship was about for me.

I know women personally that look for a man to take care of them. They want a tycoon type that can provide them with every desire. I'm not sure that is the right path to finding the person that completes you and makes you a better person. For some, that's not as important as the sense of security and the man wanting to be the provider.

Others are looking for those intangibles that come with love. Women want to be treated like a queen in the emotional/ esteem sense. It is not so much about the money and provisions.

The independent minded woman tends to put work first. When juggling the man with work and everything else, some things get dropped, and it is usually the guy. We want to continue out with what we worked so hard to achieve.

So, in choosing between the three options of the man that provides, the man that loves through the intangibles, and the independent life of continuing to achieve in my own right, I want all three. I don't want to choose between them. I want all of these things in my life, so I've been holding out for everything.

So, not just around my family, but with myself I decided it was important to be cautious with my heart, soul, and life. You should be with yours as well because you are worth it too.

Then, age 35 hit. Oh, thirty-five was a tough milestone on this front. You become ready to consider dumping all the ideals and find the minimum acceptable options. I don't want to be one of those old ladies that judges others because I never got a chance. Being the independent fifty, sixty, or seventy year old woman bitter about the life others have does not appeal to me.

"Just send someone my way," I beg God.

God gets through to me finally as He always does and He tells me that I asked for someone special. He's not just sending anyone and everyone to meet that request. Also, I have to come to grips with the fact that I'm not ready for that person. It is tough for me to face, but the truth is that I need to grow more first.

I have to work on myself and my insecurities if I ever want to be able to have a successful relationship with the man I am asking God to bring me.

I have issues of trust due to the men that have not treated me as I deserved in the past. This is an obstacle to building healthy relationships in the present. Whomever I am dating will end up paying for the sins of broken trust from those in the past, which is not his fault.

I have observed and witnessed the harm done by men who cheat. I've seen abuse and ugly break ups. I don't want to end up like those women and relationships did.

It is not bad to be single for a while - it gives you an opportunity to grow. As women we love hard and get attached quickly. I can become so focused on the person I've brought into my life, that I lose focus on myself. Other's happiness ends up taking the place of growing in my own life. As a woman who prides herself on her independence, I don't like that.

So, I am not fully ready to trust. I need to bring my insecurities to God and not into my next relationship. Until I change my mindset, I'm not giving that next relationship a real chance at success.

I do need to have love for myself and value placed on my worth. I have to truly believe that I am capable of being a good wife and partner. I need to be complete in a way that allows me to be in a healthy, beloved relationship.

Many of us are in a transition mode. We need to finish the transition. We need to become the whole person. I have to deal with this phase of my life for now.

Part of that for me is still putting importance on my career. I have personal endeavors and gifts that need to be utilized to their full potential.

We do not want to face our own need for growth as we face out looking for answers from love. Love is the solution for many problems, but it is also the reward for having taken the time to apply solutions to the areas of need in your life. The time we wait for true love is not just waiting, but working on the person we are that we bring into the relationship we seek.

For me, it will involve building a healthy sense of self-worth and learning to not be so quick to judge.

I've grown to believe that when I am ready, I will be surprised by it and love will come into my life when I least expect it. Like other aspects of my life, losing the desperation is helpful. It is not attractive professionally or personally. Maybe I won't mess it up by over thinking everything.

There is no perfect thing to say to a person that is feeling the pain of being alone. That pain, however, by itself, is not productive in bettering ourselves to be ready for the relationship we want, we deserve, and that is designed for us. Settling is not the best option no matter how far along the timeline you are. God has a timeline and His is better than ours. Do not wait passively. Work on you so that you have the best chance at the life and relationships you desire.

CHAPTER 15: MAKE TIME FOR YOURSELF

Here is an interesting and scary question for us to ponder. If those around me were asked, "What do you think about Tressa," how would they answer? What would the people around you and in your life say about who you are? If I had to guess just from observation and anecdotal conversations, I believe most people in and around my life would list qualities like strong, independent, doing it on her own, helpful, gives advice, life of the party, funny, or someone we want to include.

The interesting part of this question is that we imagine what others would say and our response actually shapes the image we think we are projecting to the world. This is a complicated layer of thinking, but there are some psychological theories that say what we think other people think of us is the most revealing about what we actually think of ourselves. It is sort of a trick to get inside your own head and see below all the protective layers at how we really shape our self-image.

The problem is that many of us shape our lives in such a way that we know the image we are putting out there to everyone is a shell we are creating for the purpose of protecting ourselves. We know that is not who we truly are, but if we do our job of image building well enough, we believe we have everyone fooled into thinking that is the real person we are. And maybe you do have them all fooled, but how much time are you taking away from the real you to keep up this public image of you?

Maintaining a "life lie" is tough work. It has all the complex issues that go with trying to keep from being caught in a lie, but it also has all the added work of maintaining separate identities. There is a lot of tough acting that goes on in a day where we have to put on for everyone around us. This may be part of the reason work exhausts us beyond all the other things that go into a job.

When I get up in the morning and go through my morning bathroom routine, I reach a point where I'm washing my face with water from the sink, and then raise my head up to look at myself in the mirror for the first time during the day. When I take that first look, I don't see the happiness I work so hard to project to everyone else.

I do put in the time to talk to myself and prepare myself mentally. I affirm and claim what I want from my day. I do this to prepare myself for success, but I'm fighting something else too. I don't see what I think others see.

What I see in those morning moments under all the false imagery is someone who is still dealing with being unhappy. I see "lack of." I see a woman who is confused and lost. She is still unsure. I see a big question mark hanging above my face.

There is so much I haven't completed or haven't started. I want more than this for myself. I'm not seeking superficial accomplishments. I am not after a list of tally marks for me to make a show of what I have accomplished. It's about building a real life. I want a fulfilling career that matches with my purpose. I want to be in a solid, loving relationship. I want to be stable financially. I want to accomplish the things I am meant to do that I haven't tried.

My coworkers have begun to figure out something is different about me. They invite me to happy hours, but every time I have a reason I can't go. I have something to do with my daughter, choir practice, I have to study, or I need to write.

They look at me like I'm making excuses. They want to know why I never want to come out anymore.

The term "sell out" has started to come up. They have their vision of what they want to do with their time and they are uncomfortable with me choosing to be outside of that. I don't want to enjoy short term fun. Long term successes are my goal now.

When people's focus is on fun, it almost always tends to center around alcohol. I have a long history of bad choices centered around the use of alcohol for fun. I need something better in my life, and I need fun that involves doing other things.

It is a bit embarrassing to have this level of conversation with any of them because they don't *want* to understand me. . That's not what I'm looking for. I am growing in a different direction from them. I'd love to say, "I'll go for only an hour," but an hour will always become something longer. I know myself, and I know that I have trouble with limits.

I hate to disappoint people, but there are obligations versus excuses. There are responsibilities that are not just excuses. I want to better myself. I need to set the example for my daughter. I need to think of my future, her future, and not what bottle is waiting around the corner offering short term fun.

We all make the mistake of building a life around others and their expectations. We put on a role to please folks. I put a lot of time into making others laugh. I put on being energetic. I give opinions to anyone that asks and some that don't like a person that is so sure of the world.

Behind closed doors, I find myself in a vulnerable mood. People don't see this side of me because I won't let them. They don't see the anxiety and panic. I stick by the old saying, "Don't ever let them see you sweat." We all want to avoid looking weak in front of others.

When we go out in public, we put on our happy masks. We hide the real person who is inside of us, who is tired and only comes out when no one is watching. That moment hits hard sometimes. It takes so much energy to make people think you have it all together.

In the corporate world, you can't show your real face. You are forced to put on a front. You have to "hide your crazy." I've had trouble at different points where my personal life slips into my work life. People made me mad, and I vocalized my emotions. When I get really mad, it makes me start crying. This stuff builds and it gets in the way of maintaining professionalism.

Once I have my make-up on, I can keep up my happy face and be the image I want to project to others in meetings.

We want to fit in and we want to belong, but that desire does not serve our real needs or the time we need for ourselves. You can't please everyone. You will kill yourself trying. That life will never truly be happy. That life is never sane and you will go crazy.

You need to see the real parts of yourself and spend time serving that person – feeding that life.

What makes you happy?

Don't think of that in terms of the small, temporary wants. What brings you fulfillment? How do we build a life that really sets us up for truly being in love? It is reasonable to want to be a homeowner and debt free. I want to give back to my parents in a meaningful way. I want to be an advocate and an active member of my community.

I know it can happen in time.

It is important to take the time for yourself. You need "vacation days." That may mean taking days off for yourself but not going anywhere. This does not necessarily mean actually using a vacation day, but it may. It may mean taking the days off you have or your hours after work to spend time on yourself. Use that time to re-evaluate. These times serve as a "life checker." Find your right path and spend time serving and feeding your true self instead of just your draining public image.

During these moments of life check, take a look at the people, places, and situations in your life – which ones do you need to keep and which ones do you need to change. Reflect on them and then reflect on your goals and vision.

A mindset change is required. You need a mindset of honesty with yourself and a mindset of victory to overcome the obstacles you've allowed to fill your path or that you put there for yourself.

It's never too late to switch paths from an unrewarding existence to the path of your purpose and dreams. We set arbitrary deadlines for ourselves instead of goals. We set age limits on our dreams and cut ourselves off from even trying after certain points. Making these changes for yourself requires a realistic evaluation of your life, but it is not cut off by age unless we choose to give up ourselves.

You may need to redefine happy hours from time out at the bar to time bettering yourself. Spend time with friends, but make choices that move you forward in life. For some of us, that does mean replacing the bar with something creative or productive in our lives. Eventually you will desire more fulfilling activities over that wasted, temporary fun.

Successful people don't surround themselves with lazy, unproductive people. They do not fill their lives with draining, unproductive activities.

A life spent on maintaining the tiresome public image is a life spent on others and not our true selves. It is a life that starves out your true self. Your life and future are worth so much more than that. Take the time to feed your spirit, better yourself, and seek out your purpose in life.

Ephesians 4:1

… I urge you to live a life worthy of the calling you have received.

CHAPTER 16: THE VALUE OF A DOLLAR

I'm a thrift shopper. I made enough mistakes in my life financially that I finally learned the value of a dollar and how to stretch it to its limit.

I coupon like crazy. Every bit saved adds up into a large amount of money saved. Money saved from necessary purchases is like additional income when it is saved and not wasted.

Even though I make more now, I still work to live below my means. I did it the other way where I bought for show and tried to keep up with the "Joneses." That lifestyle does not pay off in the end.

Saturday mornings, from time to time, I head to the thrift store. One man's trash is another man's treasure. People I see there making their dollars count are folks you would never guess would be in a place like that. I connected with a lady there that is the housewife in a very well to do family.

She said, "Even though I have money, I'm not going to burn through it."

They maintain a lifestyle because, in her case, she treats her dollars with respect.

I'm in a place now where I'm finally starting to work to get my financial life back in order.

Many people are buried under some type of financial burden. Debt, loans, credit cards, mortgages, bankruptcies and more hit people all around us without us realizing it.

Back when I was without a home, I filed bankruptcy. It is only now coming off my credit report. The total debt at that time was around sixty thousand dollars. The lawyer I was dealing with said he was used to debt in the range five hundred thousand. He said he couldn't tell me not to do it, but that there were other options besides bankruptcy.

I was embarrassed.

Looking back now, I wouldn't have handled it that way. I would have taken the time to pay it off bit by bit.

With the bankruptcy, I missed out on opportunities because of the impact on my credit. Interest rates were rough for me all those years. Even some employers do a credit check on potential candidates.

Now I sacrifice and live below my means. Then, I kept my bad habits and added more debt in addition to the bankruptcy.

Dealing with those mistakes, I use any extra money after expenses to pay down debts. If I have a hundred dollars and five creditors, I split the payment five ways and bring the debts down piece by piece.

I started small. With one debt, I spent two or three years paying an extra five or ten dollars every month. Once it got down below a hundred dollars, I started putting in more to get rid of that debt.

I don't want to knock financial counseling, but essentially you are capable of it yourself. You just have to make the commitment and muster the discipline to do it.

Creditors do not dismiss a payment. If you send them anything, they take it. You have to be disciplined to see it through. It requires a change in mindset and lifestyle, but you are investing now in a future lifestyle free of those burdens.

Creditors will give you more debt. You can have a bankruptcy or unpaid debts and you can still find someone somewhere willing to take you deeper. Don't do it. Don't follow that temptation. Dig your way back out instead.

With the bankruptcy and adding new debt on top, I was financially disabled for years. In just the last two years, my new discipline toward finances has paid off and I can see daylight again from under the burdens. I also took a Crown Financial class that was offered at my church that was very helpful in understanding debt and the biblical principles.

Some people ignore debt or rush to file bankruptcy. I didn't have someone to give me good advice through that choice. It has cost me. Don't try to keep up with the Joneses anymore. They may be in as deep as you are. They are overcharging and falling apart trying to keep up the lifestyle you are trying to imitate. It is a liberating feeling to reach the point where you don't have a problem deciding you can't afford something and just letting that unnecessary thing and the desire for it to leave your life.

CHAPTER 17: TIMING IS EVERYTHING

Things are a bit crazy right now. Aren't they always? I was in jeopardy of losing my job due to not winning any new contracts. You can't recruit anyone if you have no openings.

We didn't win new work. My coworkers wanted to stay and pretend everything was okay. I was proactively seeking out new opportunities as reality started setting in. I was in panic mode and had all the usual symptoms – pulse racing, anxiety, sweating, insomnia, etc. My daughter is going off to college. I needed to decide about renewing my lease and putting off home ownership again.

Long unemployment creates a depressive state and can perpetuate a mentality of failure and rejection that we come to accept. This is not to blame a person that is unemployed, but to recognize a struggle they face as time goes by and the situation weighs upon them.

I started actively looking and for three days I applied for every job I could find. I was putting in a dozen applications a day.

Dealing with a career, we are faced with many challenges.

In the workforce, we have to analyze our full situation and create a plan of action based on the situation we see before us. You have to weigh all the benefits and the important components that make one work situation different from another.

I applied to a particular job on a Thursday. The interview occurred on a Friday. We scheduled a follow-up interview on the next Monday which included the CEO. Then, I got the job on the spot.

This was a smaller company, so I had to work harder and couldn't just fall back on the laziness that had set in as the norm at my previous job. Sometimes we have to get out of the complacency in our current role because we get comfortable and trying new things may seem foreign to us. This job was also a twenty mile radius farther out from my home and that had to be taken into consideration as well. I was excited for the new opportunity but fearful of the new change. What if I fail at it? There I go thinking of the "What if's".

As a worker, you have to know your worth. I was offered a lower rate than what I asked, but still higher than what I was making before at my previous job. I pushed for the higher number despite my panicked, desperate mindset. If a company wants to have you and you have the skills to do what they need, they will usually be willing to meet you halfway. They met me halfway and I got higher than what they originally offered me. Look at God! Won't he do it!

I did not want to broadcast or brag about my success in finding this job. Not everyone that says they are happy for you in that situation is actually happy for you. I had the hustle mentality. Putting in ten to fifteen applications a day was a desperate act, but one that was scratching for success. After a rejection, I reached out to the hiring manager and asked him or her to keep me in mind if anything opened up later.

This was another milestone in my life. I was complacent in my previous work. I could have stayed in that relaxed environment despite all the signs that it was wiser to move on to something else. The new job would be less flexible in that regard.

With my new job, I'm in a management position with added responsibilities that challenge the skills I have already developed. I was skeptical and thought maybe this isn't what I'm supposed to do. This move took me out of my comfort zone.

In the past, when I interviewed, I prayed and asked God to give me what I was seeking. I felt like I got no answer and instead got one rejection after another.

With this job, I expanded my search. Things started coming my way. The job I ended up getting was farther out than I would normally seek. I figured I was used to rejections, so what could it hurt? I went for it. The confirmation of it all came so fast.

Then, I went back to God and asked, why this time?

We ask Him for certain things in life. We ask for what we want in the moment. We look for easy answers and an easy way out of our challenges. We want a quick relief. We also ask for a spouse, recovery from illness and troubles, blessings raining down, and other things we want in the same, rushed way.

Often things we want are not in His plan and often not on our timeframe. When we realize this, we can keep our faith and hold on for His timing. Things will manifest and things we didn't think to ask for at all will come, like this particular job outside my driving radius and outside my comfort zone.

The one job I didn't freak out about was the one I got. I got it with more and better than I had before.

The timing was significant for me in a way that is not lost on me. My old job was coming apart as this new one came open at just the right time. Before this, I wanted to be close to my daughter's school, but now she is preparing to go off to college. All of this moved me in a new direction at the only time this particular move was possible.

When you are going through a major challenge or change, and especially if you feel you have dealt with a history of failures or rejections in the past, then it is important to focus on getting it right at the right time. Don't succumb to the stress of facing yet another challenge in the light of that history. Encourage yourself through the time of waiting for something to come. It will come. If you are a spiritual person, you have to trust in that relationship with God. It requires trust. It seldom comes when exactly we expect or want, but He always will come on time.

I had looked for work at various moments in the past over the course of the years I spent at that job. I was tired of a particular situation or just tired of it all, but I got rejected when I tried to find an escape. The timing wasn't right. The handwriting was on the wall this time. I was humbled by the need to find something new and was obedient to trust God as I put in my best work to find the job I needed.

This is true for career situations, but it is true for life too. Timing is everything. You must being willing to work through rejections and fight through failures. You must be willing to put in the work during a challenge and be prepared to be in the place of success when the timing is right for you to claim it. It is a process. Do not sink into the depression that comes so easily from a series of rejections and failures. Trust that God is looking out for you through the struggles and He is prepared to see you through the successes too in His timing.

CHAPTER 18: STARTING SOMETHING NEW

My last day at my old job brings me great anxiety. It's not that I am regretting going or that I am unhappy about my new job. Ending something in life and starting something new both come with stress. There is heartache and fear. The sacrifice of leaving something behind and the struggle to begin something new are acts which test us and our faith. They are painful in the way that the act of creation is painful. Breaking down the old and building the new pushes us to our limits in every way. If it were easy, everybody would do it instead of staying with the old while letting new opportunities pass by.

As the morning of my last day started, I couldn't believe it was happening. It wasn't the first time I have left something behind to begin something new. It probably won't be the last either, and that all made me anxious.

I made my rounds through the day early and my exit interview was put off for a while. If this chapter is my real exit interview for that job with you, I can be a little more real with you about it. I would tell you that I left because there was no potential for growth. My feelings of nostalgia came from the people. It was more about the people I was leaving behind than the desk or the phone or the tasks or anything else that came with that job.

A career has to come with a path and that path has to lead up. Without a career path, you are sitting in place instead of progressing on a journey. Without career advancement, you are just doing a job or collecting a check. There is no future in that. There is barely a present and there is no past to be proud of.

In a very un-business-like sense, career paths sometimes require a person to step out on faith. Without faith, we are complacent and barely alive. When you decide to quit doing a job and start on a real career path, everything gets tested. Everything about you is on the line and is put at risk. You are taking a real gamble with your life and future serving as the chips in the pot. But if you aren't going to bet on yourself, why are you playing this game at all. This is your life. Push your chips in.

Reflecting back, I see what role this job played in my life and why it is time to bet on myself with something new.

So many people embraced me and expressed how happy they were for me. Some of them handed me their resumes and asked me to keep them in mind if anything came up where I could give them a hand up. That is quite a responsibility and adds to my anxiety a bit.

I have prayed about this new chapter of my life. My daughter is going off to college. I'm seeking to mend relationships within my family. And I'm trying to build a career as I engage my purpose for life. This litany of opportunities and changes is hitting me all at once - which is what life tends to do.

Still, you need to be prepared to decide and to act on opportunities when they come. After I lined up my new job, I had many people approaching me with questions such as, "How do I know how much to ask for?"

Ultimately, you have to know your worth. This comes from being able to objectively evaluate all you have to offer. A Lexus should not be sold at a Honda price. You need to put in the work to be the Lexus and not the Honda trying to pass itself off as something else. We sell ourselves short because we are in desperation mode.

Sometimes we settle for money or title and ignore the dead end we have walked down.

Sometimes we are battered by rejection and we give up on trying. "Why am I getting turned down?" Desperation shows. Desperation is not read well by employers and it makes them nervous about taking a chance on a person. They are taking a gamble with each hire.

At times in the past, I sounded like I was begging for a job and they saw my desperation. They took it wrong. Ironically, when I was more passively looking, I presented myself as stronger and surer, and it made employers more willing to gamble on me.

My anxiety level is high preparing for the next phase of my life and career path. I will be an HR manager. I will be running a department. My comfort zone is gone and I have to prove myself right from the beginning.

Fear of failure is high – level 10 high! What if I don't live up to it? What if I don't like the choice I have made now that it is too late to change it? These are the anxieties that come with every new beginning. Some psychologists and counselors refer to the "six month rule." Some time within the first six months after a decision, especially career decisions, whether you decide to stay with the old or to go with the new, you will come to doubt the choice you have made. This seems to hold up no matter which choice you make. Both choices eventually lead to the same form of buyer's remorse. This is why it is important to face the fear of failure that comes with choices involving new starts. We will all face self-doubt at some point.

We need the confidence to go in headfirst. Speak your success into the existence and pass through your fears as you face them. Tell yourself that you will succeed in meeting expectations. Believe that you will do work everyone can be proud of, including yourself and those watching you. Build yourself up to make it a reality.

For folks trapped in their comfort zones, take steps to break out. If you are not happy, face the change you need. If you wake up without a purpose, find it and go out looking to seize on the opportunities you need and want. If you are tired of just being a paycheck collector, then get out of the situation that is leaving you unfulfilled. Some people want to make an impact and you can do it.

Go talk to your boss. Ask him or her what your next step is in the organization. If they can't give you that next step, chances are your tenure there is expiring. You have to believe you are worth more.

I left on good terms with my old company. I still had my box full of all of my things and looked back over my shoulder at the building. I built a lot of relationships there. I thought I could maximize my potential there, but that didn't happen.

A job is not just the pay, even though that is an important part of it. You really need to look at all aspects of the situation including benefits, the commute, room for growth, work environment, and more. We often fail to analyze the whole job. The picture is bigger than one piece.

We take jobs for the wrong reasons. Finding your purpose and your future in your work and career choices is how we further ourselves in that regard. That's when we find success.

Leaving an old relationship of any kind to start something new is a test. We can get what we seek out and ask for in life. You will be able to grow if you put yourself where you belong and where you need to be.

CHAPTER 19: ANXIETY TAKEOVER

The Anxiety and Depression Association of America says that anxiety and depression disorders are the most common mental illnesses in the United States, affecting 40,000,000 adults and accounting for 18% of the population. That is one out of every five American adults (who have reported). My guess is that many more might be affected, but they mask their symptoms from others.

My struggles with anxiety and depression stretch back through much of my life. After my aunt was killed, I believe I sank into a depressive state much deeper than basic anxiety. Many of us do for a wide range of reasons. We think we are not pretty enough or not good enough and we let those ideas sink in deep.

I feared that if I stayed in my hometown, things would not change. In addition to battling my depression at that time, I feared that I would end up with multiple kids and a minimal job. I feared I would end up strung out on something. In small towns, there is not always much to do. It is easy to look for trouble when you are down and short on options; and, it is easy to find trouble when you start looking. I also feared I would end up dead at an early age in that small town. I would have stuck around in an abusive relationship or found some other path to do myself in. I'm fairly certain of all this.

Sometimes we go through some hard paths and difficult choices to find our greater angels. Even when we look back on our lives, it is tough to figure out how we overcame some things. There is hard work and choices to fight our way out. There are also other factors that seem to indicate that there are forces out there reaching down to pull us up. We can try to do it all on our own, but it is good to take a helping hand from outside ourselves. That might be a person who offers help when help is needed or that might be a spiritual hand that lifts us up in ways we might not be able to clearly see at the time.

No one told me to leave my hometown. That message came to me from within in some way. In my depression, that was my hard road out. I didn't want to be in the light. I wanted to be in the dark all the time. I wanted to find the smallest space I could with a door so I could close on myself. I needed closed doors and four walls around me. That's definitely not always easy when a person is homeless though.

I did not have the same relationship with God back then that I do now. He was still reaching His hand down to lift me up and set me on a path back to Him, but I was not attuned to His voice or His guidance at the time. As I get older, I understand better how I was being watched and lifted. I see my hard road from a few miles farther along and some of those rough patches make more sense now than when I was in the midst of walking them. Seeing that journey behind me helps me to better understand the rough patches I walk now. I know that I'm being watched and lifted even now. I know that from a few miles farther along, my walk now will make more sense. I take great comfort in that even as I deal with my anxieties now.

I sought help. Doctors wanted to put me on medication, which, when handled properly, can be part of that helping hand to lift us up and out. I was around people that took pills to excess though. Environment can go a long way to help or to hurt in our struggles. In small towns, it was weed and drinking. In corporate America, it was prescription pills.

The behind the scene stresses were an easy drive for people in those corporate environments to abuse medication in that way. In the call center where I worked at that time, there were stresses to get those orders ready and out. Those stresses increased as I was promoted and had sales quotas for all the people taking the orders from customers under me. I was in my twenties and looking at other management around me in their thirties and forties that were already graying and showing age beyond their years due to stress. Stress takes a toll on our bodies.

It was a bit of a high for me. My depression switched over to anxieties. I dealt with it by meeting up with people and going out to clubs to party and celebrate. I was constantly either building up steam under the endless pressure of work or letting off steam through my questionable choices outside of work.

The water cooler talk about the stresses and how they dealt with them fueled this self-medicating and over self-medicating environment. They got stressed out and then they popped the pills. If someone pissed them off, they took a pill to level out. I was given a Xanax one day by a well-meaning co-worker that I took on top off coffee, mixing the upper with the downer reaction. In the end, no one could make me mad and I rode that feeling through the day.

My anxiety level finally began to kick up until I was forgetting basic things I needed to get done. I feared losing my job. I didn't have time to get done what I needed to during the day. I'd forget to pay a bill and I'd shutdown other areas of my life as I got too overwhelmed.

My doctors kept switching me from one drug to another trying to balance me out. Each change over added more stress and side effects. Wellbutrin was first. Then they switched me to Zoloft. I had a bad reaction to that. They moved me to Paxil after that and so on.

Doctors kept prescribing instead of looking at the root problem. About fifteen years ago, I ended up with a psychiatrist. I asked myself who this person was. I was not opening up completely or giving my all. I told her what she wanted to hear.

I would take what was prescribed for a while and then stop. From my environment and background and with all I had going on, I feared dependency. My anxiety came and went. I had good days and bad days.

The crazy thing looking back is that even when I was homeless, my anxiety levels were the least. At that time in my life, I was struggling with shame and embarrassment over my situation. I was in survival mode. Everything else was shut out at that time. I had depression hanging over me, but I was focused on more simple and basic things.

Later on, when I got my life together and ended up in Washington D.C., I was always finding myself in high stress roles. I was trying to do eight or ten tasks at a time. Or maybe I thought I was expected to. My anxiety came back in force in that setting. The anxiety would come and go. I never could completely get rid of it though.

I want people to understand that these struggles are often connected to triggers. My stressors would trigger panic attacks in me. I'd get heart palpitations. I was scared to close my eyes for fear that I wouldn't wake up again. I would force myself to stay up because of this fear. This was like drug addict behavior and it could become extremely destructive if allowed to go on unchecked. I was still taking back to back cups of coffee through the night to keep myself awake during these moments of fear.

I went back to the doctor. As my daughter went off to college and I became aware that fear of sending her away to school wasn't the only part of my stress, I knew I needed to get control of the situation again. I went to see the doctor more often at this point in my life than ever before. Having my life back was more important to me than ever. With my physical symptoms, I wanted to be certain that everything was all right physically. The doctor assured me that my symptoms were anxiety related and we could deal with them in that way.

I asked him, how do I cope? I was worried about dependency again. I didn't want to risk the side effects of suicidal tendencies from withdrawing off certain medicines. The doctor reassured me that I wasn't becoming dependent because I wasn't coming back for refills over and over like some patients did. That is the definition of taking a medicine as needed apparently.

We get by through willpower and the grace of God sometimes. I've added to my resolve recently through meditation and prayer. I'm writing more. I'm writing this book, but also other pieces and poems to express my feelings.

My anxiety comes from trying to finish too many things at once sometimes. I have to scale back for my own health. I learn to say "no" more strategically. I'm quick to say "yes" too often. If I don't take on the extra tasks, I can focus my energy on those things that matter. With my daughter, my job, my church, and responsibilities back home, I could say "yes" to more things than a human being could possibly do. I can't always say "yes."

Doing things outside of my triggers has helped too. I used to get stressed and I would go work. Work was my trigger, so I was just adding on. Here is where that prayer and meditation came in. Even if you don't consider yourself a spiritual person, meditation practices can help you step away from some of your triggers. Turning television and social media off can ease your mind and help you to reset. Giving yourself time for activities away can build you up to deal with the stresses in a more powerful way.

You are not alone in this. Many people know how you feel and many people are ready to help. Even on the roughest stretch of your road, there is a helping hand reaching to lift you up. You will make it to the road ahead of this time and look back at how far you have come with amazement.

CHAPTER 20: STAY FOCUSED

Even during trials and tribulations, I'm left to juggle all the pieces and problems in my life. Trying new things brings new challenges and can quickly pile up. The key for me is to remain focused. Staying focused and organized is one of my lifelong weaknesses.

I have been blessed with a creative mind and creative ideas. I have been cursed with the desire to rush into each new idea I have. Excitement is good, but becoming excited about too many things at once can be a problem for both focus and organization.

My mind goes a mile a minute and tends to speed up when I'm excited about something new. When I start something new, my focus drops somewhere and I tend to find failure.

In my earlier twenties, I tried to start a women's group, planning nightlife and social events, writing articles, going back to school, juggling career goals, hanging out with friends and still trying to be the best mom I could be. Some of these things needed to be higher priorities than others, but I tried them all at once. I met initial success with each and that fueled my excitement. As each endeavor suffered because my priorities were not in order, many met roadblocks, disorganization, and failure.

Someone wasn't getting enough attention. None of them were organized well enough. Priority was my daughter first but it was easy to get consume with the other 99 tasks that she would at times suffer in terms of not getting enough attention from me.

Fast forwarding to today, I realize I have to approach my goals differently to find success. I can't juggle five, six, or seven things at once. I can't organize everything all at once and expect to find success in everything.

My priorities are different now. My daughter is visiting colleges and preparing to head out into that phase of her life. I'm more active in the ministries of my church and working to succeed at a new job and finishing this book. It would be very easy to pile on again and steal focus from these priorities. It's a lot, and for a split second I began to feel the panic I remember from ten years ago.

God puts people in your life for a reason. He reveals things in His own way and in His own time. Often, he reveals things that people don't realize He is revealing and not in the way they think or expect.

I was telling my boss about all these things going on in my life and how I was writing this book as well. She said to me, "Tressa, you are all over the place. You need to focus. Deal with one thing at a time. Your focus should be on things that advance your career and earn you more money. Think about finishing school and being a success at this career."

Understandably, her thought was a focus on career. She saw priority as things which advance my income to six figures and continue to work for her to make sure the department is ran smoothly.

I thought about it. Focus on my career? Okay. That sounds like good advice. Going back to school is usually a good idea, it was something I've meant to do for a while, and it would help my career. Maybe that is what I should be doing.

Is that my priority? I have a tendency to grab onto the ideas others present to me. It is my instinct to hear it, process it, and run to achieve it. That has not always led me to focusing and organizing around my highest priorities though. STOP allowing others to dictate your future. You have the power to create your own vision.

I'm quick to gravitate toward others' opinions. God used her to bring a message to me, but not the one she thought. The message I got was that I need to focus on my highest priorities.

Because I come from a spiritual background, my filter is set to considering what God's priorities are for my life. My pastor was speaking the other day and he said, "We need to be doing more to step out on faith more often. God expects us to live up to our purpose designed by Him."

When I am at my job, I don't think about my job most. I am more attuned to other things that I believe align to my purpose. I believe I do a good job, but that place is not my purpose. Other things are aligned to my calling in life.

I believe I am called to use my voice. My purpose, my priorities, and my focus are on writing, speaking, and helping others.

Everything else around me is starting to transform. Doors are opening for other things and new opportunities. I don't want to move backward. I have to trust God first and I need to stop letting my mind be all over the place.

I spoke at my church recently. The topic was to be about what the church has meant to me. When I got up, I was moved in a different direction though. I had prayed about it beforehand and thought I knew what I was going to say when I got up, but the Spirit led me in an entirely different direction.

I talked about my struggles. I talked about sleeping in my car and how God has brought me to where I am now. I talked about living from paycheck to paycheck. By the time I was finished, I had shared the direction of my life and what I believe to be my purpose in using my voice to share my struggles to help others. My purpose had never been clearer to me and my priorities never more organized before me. The reaction of those hearing my truth served as a confirmation for my journey. Here, I was given a glimpse of my calling in life and the future ahead of me.

That was the reason I was supposed to give that testimony. My spirit is telling me to focus on my gifts.

I've decided I have to focus on finishing the key project represented by this book and meeting my purpose in life. Seeking God first on a daily basis in my decision making and asking for clarity to stay on a focused track.

CHAPTER 21: BREAKING THE CURSE

God has something bigger in store for me and lessons for me to learn before I get there. My spirit is leading me to share something very personal. I believe God is calling me to be fully transparent to serve others through my story.

I have spoken of this weight that hangs heavy above my family and presses down on our backs and shoulders. I have told of what my grandmother, my mother, and I went through with each of our own struggles. We speak of it as a generational curse which represents the consequences of the bad choices we have made. I fear for my daughter for this reason. Whether we believe in this curse as a real force in our life is beside the point. History repeats itself. That we all know to be true. The challenge is to be a different mother to give my daughter a different chance for a different life.

It is past time to break the curse.

My senior year I hid the truth from my mother. I was pregnant and I hid that fact for months until I couldn't hide it any longer.

All my behaviors led to consequences and I fear for my daughter repeating my choices. All the lying and hiding is easy for teens to fall into.

I told my mother I was going to countless "sleepovers" when I was really doing other things. I was willing to give my time and myself to anyone who told me I was cute.

I was pregnant at my prom. I was pregnant when I crossed the stage at my graduation. As my classmates and I talked about college and the next chapter in our lives, I knew I would not be able to attend and I hid it because it was easier to go on lying. I wrapped tampons and maxi pads and threw them in the trashcan to maintain my lie as long as possible.

This brings me forward to today.

I was at work like normal. However, after my daughter's recent doctor's visit, it came to my attention that we were going to have to have a discussion about changing course before she made the same mistakes I did. She has not yet, but it is her senior year and she appears to be trying very hard to repeat history. I thought we had an open line of communication, I assumed we had talked enough about choices, and I believed that she was being honest with me; but, it appears I wasn't completely correct on all those points.

As a single mother who made these mistakes, I'm stricken with fear of my daughter repeating them. I feel what my mother felt when she named this pattern our family generational curse. I can't be satisfied to stumble and submit to that fate though. There is still time to begin a path of different choices. I thought we were there, but I find that the work of breaking the curse isn't yet done. I'm thankful to have the chance and the knowledge that it still needs to be done, but I am also overwhelmed and stricken by the task. I was rebellious as a child, I told elaborate lies, and history was trying to repeat itself.

It feels like too much for me and it probably is. I have to depend on God to guide me and I have a few things to ask forgiveness for as well.

It was 2:15 and I was still at work. I was emotional and everything in front of me became a blur. I was unfocused and shaking. My daughter was not exactly who I thought she was and I didn't know what to do with that. I felt the weight and guilt of what I had put my mother through and it was paralyzing me as a mother now.

I went into my boss's office at a job I had just begun. You don't want to let your emotions show in a professional setting, especially early on, but I was overwhelmed. I told her enough to let her know I had a problem that required me to leave early. I offered to work extra hours or weekends to make it up. She told me to take tomorrow off as well. My emotions and stress must have been showing far more than I thought.

So, I went home.

Kids experiment and I know as well or better than anyone that they do not consider the consequences. They do not fully understand the cost until it is too late and a part of their future has been stolen from them. My daughter does not see the hurt she is causing herself and others with these choices. She sure does not see the full danger either.

Doing the right things as a parent never guarantees things will work out perfectly. It does not spare you from the struggles. It does not eliminate the dangers. No parent especially a mother want to hear that their daughter has experienced adulthood at an early age. Was my one on one conversations not effective enough? What could I have done differently to prevent this from happening?

I am putting my words together in a clear fashion right now, but I exploded at my daughter. I cussed at her. It was not a good scene. She went upstairs to be by herself and we had solved nothing. As mothers it is in our nature to protect our own from hurt, danger, and anything else that is no value that will hinder their potential. We know what it is like in life to be vulnerable and the longing of wanting to be accepted. My mother had my brother when she was thirteen and she would always be firm with me for a reason. At the time I didn't understand but as I got older and had my own child then it all made sense of the overbearing and constant reminders from her.

I got myself together and I apologized. We started a conversation, but we are far from finished. I offered to go to counseling together so that we can build trust, have some important discussions, and work out some issues that have been unaddressed for a while. Even though I offered it was never followed through.

Without her father being here every day as a part of her life, she has it harder than I did in a way. This can push her toward guys that are not good for her. It also leaves me to deal with it all as the sole parent. If I suggest involving her father in any way, that holds no meaning to her.

We have to be willing to seek out the help and support we need to get through the struggles of life. As I seek to help others, I still need to seek help for myself and my family. I am thankful we discovered the needed to have this discussion before history fully repeated. Though I am hurt, it is an opportunity to break the curse. Breaking curses is a painful undertaking, but the struggle is better than living under the darkness of curses any longer.

Discussing this brings up fear and shame in me. I do not want my friends to know my baggage, but truth is important for the people closest to me and those I do not know who are reading this and need to hear it. Pulling back the illusion that we are perfect is uncomfortable, but necessary. Otherwise, I am still the dumb girl trying to hide something that can't stay hidden. I do not want to be living backwards any longer.

Sometimes we have to be broken in order to get our breakthrough. I told her that I loved her and that I was sorry for many of the things I said. I assured her that I was here to help her through whether she liked it or not. We are in this together and we will work toward better choices and a positive future as a team.

CHAPTER 22: LEARNED LESSONS

While I haven't disclosed everything yet, it is appropriate for me to tell this story of struggle now. It fits well here after the point where I am dealing with helping my daughter to make better choices.

There are things I don't know if people should know about me. It hurts to tell it. After all these years, it still hurts. I tell it now to help many of you and I tell it because I told my daughter this to help her avoid my mistakes.

I had a car accident my junior year that could have been easily avoided. My mother got the call and she said, "No, that can't be my daughter in the hospital. She is at church."

Well, of course, it was me. I wasn't where she thought I was, I wasn't doing what she thought I was doing, and I suppose I wasn't really the person she thought I was. I made my grades and had the look of being an upstanding teen, but that did not save me from making big mistakes with consequences I was not ready to face at that age. Not having the courage to tell my mom the truth that I wanted to sneak out and hang out with my boyfriend doing adult things was not an option to disclose

This incident sums up the problem with the lies and lack of communication that led to me being in a place to make bad choices. I didn't have the extra focus on me with my parents' attention divided among other things.

I got pregnant my senior year and became a single mother with my daughter. That was not my only pregnancy and not my first pregnancy that year. It was November of my senior year. I was afraid. My mom was church-going and I saw her as holier-than-thou despite all she had done in her life.

The guy I was with at that time jumped immediately to abortion as a solution. I took no other advice and I decided to go that route.

This was the 1990's and abortion was a tougher prospect then than even now. It is a more discrete experience now. I lived in Virginia, and it was a parent consent state. My boyfriend drove me to Greensboro, North Carolina.

The day we went to the clinic, I started by going to school like a normal day. I got out for an early release and left with my boyfriend for the forty mile trip.

When we got there, it was an unmarked building. It looked like any other plain office building. If we didn't know where we were going, we would have never found it. It looked like no kind of medical building.

It was a Thursday, we got there early, and we were the first folks inside.

It cost $260.

As a teen, I made an adult decision. I had no parental feedback. I was numb emotionally and physically through the whole thing – maybe spiritually too. I just wanted to put it behind me and go right back to normal life.

I had a game that night. My boyfriend was a basketball player for our school and I was a cheerleader. We both wanted to get back and live our lives.

As we went back out to his car, the parking lot had filled in all the time we had been in there. In the 1990s, protestors were more common outside the clinics and more aggressive. They were not there when we arrived because it was early in the day. When we left, they were loud and everywhere. They had signs and they surrounded the car as we got inside. They beat on our windows and yelled. "Murderer!"

Others shouted. "You're going to Hell!"

They were banging on the windows and I shouted at my boyfriend, "Go! Go!"

He drove out of the parking lot and away from them. We were silent the entire trip back. I was feeling rough physically from the experience. After the protestors, I was wrung out in every other way too. I was so afraid and shaken from what I saw and what they said. The drive back was different from the drive there.

He went home and got ready to play basketball. I dressed out for cheerleading. He was able to go on like nothing happened. He was free of the physical effects, obviously, but he felt free emotionally too. He had gotten away with it.

For me, it was different. I was still bleeding, but also I was shaken to my core and not just from the threatening actions of the protestors. My own spirit and conscience were not clear of my choice.

I was still hurting physically and in my soul. By the third quarter, I had taken all I was able. I pretended to be dizzy and feeling faint. The coach let me sit out the rest of the game. I would become very good at pretending. That wasn't the first time I had lied to cover up my choices and it wouldn't be the last.

I had taken a life.

I respect anyone's view on this difficult topic, but this is mine. I made a choice that day and that choice cost a life – a life that would have been my son. He never came into this world. His life ended before he was given a chance to start. I moved on by going right back into the life I was living before, but that choice stayed with me. It hung heavy on my soul - and still does.

God forgives. People judge after God grants forgiveness, but God forgives. His hand is on our lives and He weaves our terrible choices into His plan in ways we can never understand. His grace is extended to those who do not deserve it, which is all of us. All any of us can do is accept His forgiveness and live in the grace He extends. If you made a choice you regret, this same one or any other, that is what you need to do today. It is our only redemption. That goes for all of us.

This is why I couldn't do it again. I got pregnant a second time five months later.

"I can't do it again."

His response was, "Then, you will do this alone."

"Fine."

I was still a stupid girl. I still tried to pretend like it wasn't happening half the time and the other half I thought he was going to change his mind, we were going to live a beautiful life together, and get the beautiful house with American Dream written all over it.

Doing it again would have allowed me to go on. I would have gone to college and continued the same life I was living. A lot of girls were doing the same thing. I had friends that had back-to-back abortions.

My soul said I couldn't do it again.

I feel like I can share this to honor God's grace and forgiveness. I can share it to help others struggling with the toughest choices of all.

The whole pregnancy I worried for my child's health. I thought there might be some punishment or cost from my first choice. Maybe I was going to learn a lesson from my first choice or maybe they had done something wrong during the procedure and the second baby was going to pay for it. I didn't know, but I worried.

I even went on the senior field trip to the amusement park. I rode the rides like nothing was different. I was in some state of confused denial for sure. I was on a roller coaster when reality crashed in on me finally. It was one of those that went backwards for the second half. As we went backwards, I felt like I had a basketball in my belly. I just held on and waited for it to be over. In a way, that's exactly what I was doing with my life and all my bad choices.

My daughter turned out fine, thank God.

I told this to my daughter. She was shocked, of course. She pointed out that if I had gone ahead and had my first child from my first pregnancy, she would not have been born. We never know, but that is likely true.

This is a tough lesson for many, but our bad choices do not have the power to destroy God's will. His hand is on our lives and on this world through the good and the bad. He controls it all. My life destroying choice did not remove God's power. It did not destroy His will. He was not pleased with my actions, but He was with me, He still had a plan for me, and He is still willing to forgive and use me now. He has grace to allow me the opportunity to help my daughter with her choices now – maybe you too.

I could ask God, "Are you punishing me?"

But the better response is, "Thank you for this chance to help others to make a different, better choice."

My mother did not find out about the abortion until years later. Even as I write this, many others in my life still don't know. I needed to open up to my daughter to save her from a life of hiding that leads to a painful, backward ride just holding on waiting for it all to be over. I am so humbled and thankful for the chance to guide her away from that. Whatever happens, this moment is a gift as all moments are in their way. I hope many of you read this in time to either consider a different choice or to know that forgiveness is still available.

Society is going to judge. Forgiveness is not just an option; it is needed by all of us.

CHAPTER 23: SUCCESS DESPITE OBSTACLES

Success comes with obstacles. Any achievements in life that come with no struggle at all can hardly be called achievements. They are not valued the same way and those gains are soon lost by the person who did not go through enough fight to appreciate them.

My life feels like a rollercoaster sometimes. In those moments, I wish I could get off the ride and sit by the side, just catching my breath for a little while. In real life, roller coasters just go in wild circles that get us nowhere. Some of us have been on those kinds of rides in life for a long time. Often it is our own fault and the result of our own choices. Sometimes, though, our roller coaster is really a rough road that is actually leading us somewhere. We still want to escape, but sometimes that rough ride is the only path to the success we want. We will appreciate the destination when the journey is tough.

This past summer I was moving through a bit of a high point in my life. I was trying to finish this book, I had speaking engagements, and I started a new job. Then, it seemed to come crashing down on me. The weight of the responsibility and the pressure of seeing the tough journey through caught up with me. This was the struggle that preceded my success. This was the part of the process that was harder to appreciate in the moment.

At my new job, I was the only one in the Human Resources Department of a small company. So much is required of me. In a situation like that, they don't look at it as "you might need some help," but instead, they see it as "you should be able to handle it."

My co-workers have been understanding of my personal needs. As my daughter prepared for college in the first ninety days of my new job, they still gave me time off to go do college visits with her. Still, all the work is there for my one person HR department when I get back.

My daughter is considering colleges hours away from home. I want her in the suburbs, but she is looking at schools in the cities. All of this is added pressure as I worry about her and her future. Even being a success at so many things in her life, I still have to deal with some typical teenage nonsense with her from time to time.

With all of this going on, I had low energy and felt like I had no time. Ten to twelve hour days can suck out all your energy. There feels like there is no time to catch up around the house. There is so little time to spend with my daughter like I really want. One can feel guilty for falling short on any of these areas when there just doesn't seem to be enough time in the day.

Balance is tough to find, but we can't survive without it. I skipped church the last couple of Sundays. This may not seem like a big deal for some, but worship matters to me. It feels like I'm letting go of the things that matter to me the most. I am tired and it is tempting to let certain things slide just to buy time to breathe.

Working people in our world today are hard pressed to find any balance at all. Overnight successes do exist. Sometimes that is about seizing on an opportunity. Sometimes it is being lucky enough to be first on the rising wave of a new movement. There is danger in quick success though. Quicker up is quicker down in some cases.

Hard work to reach success is more common and provides a certain durability and sustainability to success. It can give a person the tools to hold on to what they gained. It can also help a person to bounce back when things fall apart from time to time.

Sean "Puffy" Combs responded to the question "How are you so successful?" in an interesting way. He had his own clothing line, reality show, music career, restaurants, producer credits, and more. He answered, "Sleep is forbidden." P Diddy claims that for much of his rise to success, he slept two hours a night or less. This speaks to sacrifice, priorities, dedication, and hard work. He may also be crazy for giving up that much sleep; but if so, he is crazy successful.

Now I need my sleep and dropping to less than two hours of sleep a night is probably terrible advice for balance in life and for a person's health. His willingness to do what others can't or won't do is probably a huge factor in his success though. No matter what we choose to do, success requires some sacrifices. Balance in life is achieved by giving up some things to give more important things more space. Trying to do everything is where the imbalance comes into play.

In trying to do everything in my life, I started to put this book on the back burner. It was an important part of me finding my balance and serving my purpose in life, but I felt tired. I wanted to buy myself space and it was tempting to let a higher priority go in order to serve my own comfort.

I felt myself trying to slide back into old habits. Instead of acting how I used to, I had to come back to it and see this important part of my journey through.

I also had to encourage myself through the obstacles in my path. It is great to get validation from others. I crave that probably more than I should, but I need to take time to validate myself too. We are our own worst critics at the times in our lives when we need encouragement the most. We tear ourselves down and we deny ourselves acceptance even when others are acknowledging our achievements. We need to watch the type and level of criticism we pour on ourselves and instead, take the time to encourage ourselves. We need it from ourselves more than we need it from anyone else. Motivate yourself to bring your dreams out of your head and into reality. Others can limit us, but we do it to ourselves too. NOTE: Take 10 minutes each morning and give yourself a pep talk. Encourage yourself.

Part of my struggle with the pressure to finish and succeed with this purpose is that I shared it with the world in advance. That can be helpful in being held accountable, but it can have its downsides too. I put the knowledge of this project out in the atmosphere and people were asking about it. My pause became the risk of another false start. I ran the risk of appearing to be doing what I always do: starting something I'm not prepared to finish. That adds pressure and it is tempting to let it go so that pressure can ease off.

After ninety days at my new job, I got a raise. Part of the evaluation involved my boss reminding me to "focus, focus, and focus." I had shared some of what I had going on with her in the past and her response was that I should focus on my career, of course. The things that will advance me financially and make me money should be my priority. Other activities just get in the way in her mind. Sustaining my life, food on the table and clothes on my back, should be my top priorities. Hard to argue with that logic, I suppose.

I stopped talking about all of this at work some time back for that reason. Some parts of your life don't fit in some places. Certain contexts and certain people are not in a position to accept or promote your top priorities. It does not make them bad people, but it does make them the wrong people to share those parts of your life. At work especially, if you share priorities that are not compatible with their view, they will begin to associate any shortcomings, even minor slip-ups, with those priorities. It could be small, but it could also be enough to create real problems for you where professional distance might serve you a little better. Keeping those parts of your life from those people isn't lying or dishonesty. That is just not the time, the place, or the people to share that part of your life.

In this case, I have to tell myself to write instead of talking about writing. It has to be a part of my life that is private and involving the work itself instead of something I share with everyone at this point. The book of Matthew chapter 6, verse 4, talks about not letting your left hand know what your right hand is doing. In the context of that scripture, it is talking about helping the needy and committing acts of kindness. Rewards in Heaven are gained by not running around bragging about acts of kindness, but just doing them quietly for God to see. That is important for motivation and sincerity of our actions. I think, by extension, the hard work we do to achieve something is benefited by the same process. We don't share what we are trying to accomplish to get early praise, but focus on doing the work to achieve the goal. By not making it about what people see, the reward comes from moving through the tough parts of the journey to the success.

So, I need to work on doing it and not just announcing that I'm doing it. I don't need to prove anything to others, but just do the work. In most cases, people that need me to prove myself to them aren't worth convincing. Finishing the work and achieving the success is the best proof anyway. I have to stop talking about it and just be about it.

It is also not best for me to share everything just yet. If I have a history of starting and not finishing things, it is better for me to actually finish. More finishing and less talking is what I need. Otherwise, I'm constantly telling people, "I'm getting there. I'm getting there." It might be mostly true, but it is discouraging to me and them. It feeds the old pattern of starting and not finishing.

Life lived trying to accomplish the things you want most can be overwhelming. I tell myself to get it together. I remind myself that everything I am doing, everything I have been called to do, is outside my comfort zone.

I went one-on-one with God earlier this year. I had my Jacob to Israel moment. I wrestled with God with all the things that have been holding me back until God broke through to me. I decided with Him in that struggle of discovering my purpose that I did not want to live another empty year of the same old thing. I wanted to face the struggle to excel and succeed.

It is not too late to continue that journey. We are tempted to back off our struggles and give ourselves permission to strive later. We say we'll pick it back up at another time, but that's the formula that leads to failure in diets and in everything else. Mistakes and trials can knock us down or get us off track, but don't let that be an ultimate failure. Don't use those moments to buy time for failure.

Instead, pick up with the new day and keep going. Tomorrow is not promised and you can keep promising to start tomorrow without ever actually starting. Don't put it off.

If I had the power to reorder the situations in my life and my past, I would most likely be tempted to do so. There are times I wish I could turn back the hands of time. I might do something different. We have to use this desire and motivation to direct us to make different choices for our future.

Opportunities tend to present you a path to the next level and out of our comfort zones. I wanted to stay in my safe haven, but that was not where my next level was found. God has a way of stretching us.

At my new job, way out of my safe haven, I felt that pressure. I had two meltdowns of sorts. I cried and felt overwhelmed and inadequate for the task. There was so much to swallow at work. What did I get myself into? But I can't be complacent any longer. I have to be so much more than I've allowed myself to be in the past.

As with anything we have to face, I take these challenges one day at a time. I adjust some things to balance my life and serve my priorities. Sacrifices are called for to make time for what we value in life. That gives us the position and the resources we need to face the rough road and the challenging journey full of obstacles which leads to our real success in life.

CHAPTER 24: LIVE LIFE LIKE IT IS GOLDEN

I have talked a good bit in earlier chapters about my struggles and challenges being a single mother. I've also talked a lot about facing the reality of her going off to college. It seems only fair to let you in on my thoughts and feelings as the day to go off to school finally arrived. As she went off to school, I knew this moment was life changing for her as well as me of course. I did not fully realize how pivotal this was for me in those moments. I wasn't ready to grasp the fact that my baby girl would be leaving the nest. I wanted her to stay and go to school locally for my own selfish reasons. I would argue that financially it made sense to go to a community college for 2 years and then venture off, but the mother hen in me wanted to keep her close as added protection and guidance. Her decision to go away to college that was four hours away was a constant reminder that I couldn't keep her from exploring life's journey. I didn't have the option to go away to go to college because I was pregnant my senior year, but I also wasn't forced and encouraged either to go.

I have always had to be the nag. I've been on top of her schooling, behavior, and choices throughout her life. I was there to guide her and to point out bad choices or to help her avoid them entirely. She did normal teenage stuff. The little mistakes ran me ragged with worry sometimes, but I was ever watchful with her. She has worked since she was sixteen and knew the value of a dollar early on. I was particularly focused on helping her avoid mistakes. I didn't want her to be like me. I wanted her to be better than me.

I knew she was growing into a young woman. She was learning how to open a bank account and how to change her mailing address. She wanted freedom to date and party. I still wanted to maintain control over her life for her protection even as I knew she would have the power to make those choices for herself as she went off to school.

She had a curfew of 12:30 at the latest, even as a senior. There is no good to be had at her age after that time. I made her come on home after prom as well. There was not going to be extra temptation to make the same big mistakes I had made.

I knew my power was slipping as the day to move into college approached. She ended up selecting a school that was three-and-a-half hours away instead of thirty minutes away. I can still get to her, if she needs me, but she isn't under my roof or able to hop home in a moment.

I accepted her moving farther away than I original thought she would. It is a predominately black college. I had envisioned a different school with a different level of diversity. It wasn't my place or intent to try to orchestrate her college experience. Still, I pictured something different for her. And I pictured it being closer to home. That was a key piece of the picture in my mind.

We rented an SUV to get her moved up and got a hotel room for the night before the morning of check in. It was moving day and we were both heading into a new chapter of our lives.

Watching her navigate the campus and set herself up in her new life was amazing to watch. As we were walking back to the car to see me off, it really started to sink in just as you would expect it to. Of course, she was just fine.

We did the hug and selfie by the car.

She was ready to take the step past my direct reach. It would have been selfish for me to keep her home just for my piece of mind in continuing to watch over her. Staying under my roof was not what was meant for her.

I realized all of this as I watched her walk away. I held it together until I was driving across the bridge alone. I'll admit it. I cried. It wasn't just sadness; it was a sense of accomplish at having gotten her further than I had made it myself at her age. She was taking a step beyond my reach, but she was taking a step further than what I ever got to experience.

There was such a long time in my life that I thought we were never going to make it to that day living paycheck to paycheck. I know other single mothers have been through the same thing and have dealt with the same fears. I feared not being able to afford it or not being able to qualify for the aid she needed. It was scary.

Sometimes you have to get knocked down before you can get back up. I cried myself to sleep a few nights, wrapping my brain around this monumental change in my life. Of course, she wasn't crying. I called her and she was doing just fine.

I check in on her. I'm still worried. I know she has temptations there. She is exposed to things I was able to shelter her from here at home.

I tell her "I love you" as much as I can. I tell her every chance I get. I don't think she doubts it or will forget, but I think it is good for her to hear and for me to say.

She's starting to be herself more around me and over the phone. She's letting her guard down in conversations and opening up more than she seemed to do before. I'm starting to see a hint of the woman she is eventually going to grow to be – that she is meant to be.

I have to trust that she heard and took with her what I have said over the years. Mistakes will be something she makes in life and will have to live with. I can't do it for her as much as I might like to.

I pray for her. If I do that, I know I have to trust God with it. I can worry, but worry is a sin. I have to trust that God will watch over her. She still has free will, but I have to believe that He is watching and hearing my prayers.

She told me that she and her friends went out to a party at another college. Her friends wanted to stay, but she didn't feel comfortable. She and her roommate went ahead and left early. They took an Uber back to campus. I was proud of her. These are the signs of maturity that make me feel better about who she is becoming and that she is ready to move that direction.

The last few days, I've been trying to occupy my time to keep myself from focusing on the things that will make me worry. It's hard not to feel like something is missing as the house seems so empty sometimes.

I need to stay in contact with her not just by phone conversations, but in terms of our relationship. I want no generational curse pulling us apart or bringing us to a point that we aren't able to share our lives with each other. I think this is important for both of us.

I try to be respectful around older generations in my family, but I also hide aspects of myself and my life from them. I don't think that has been positive for any of us.

I'm not seeking to repeat that relationship pattern.

This whole experience and transition was a wake up call for me.

I realized that I was moving into a phase of returning to the idea of finishing what I have started. I still have life in me and I was losing my excuses for holding back in fulfilling my purpose.

I still have a desire to start traveling and seeing places I have not experienced before. I want to experience life.

How do I teach my daughter to reach out and find success, if I behave like I am afraid to do so myself? I can't. I need to step out and use my life in this new chapter as well. We have to live our lives like they are golden. Life is that precious and the time we spend is too precious to waste.

I have to bring myself to take the next steps for my life, journey, and purpose. We each have to be ourselves and we have to be our best selves by seeking out our purpose in life. As this time period opens up in my life, I'm going to use it as a launching point for my own personal growth. My daughter and I both are taking steps into great new chapters in our lives that we worked hard to achieve for a very long time.

CHAPTER 25: TAKING TIME

Parenting is challenging, but that doesn't really sum up the experience. It can be a struggle, but it is not exactly a hurdle or an obstacle. Parenting can be a very isolating experience during the key moments of the struggles. Communication would go a long way in helping to deal with these challenges and struggles.

Time would help too. Parenting is one of those life commitments that absorbs all your time. The truth is that everything we do in life will eat up as much time as we allow these things to. The key is to take back the time to live your life to the fullest. Your life fills the time you have.

I wish I had a roadmap to raising a daughter for all those years. The challenges through the years sometimes caught me on my heels, and I spent a lot of time trying to play catch up.

I got pregnant for all the wrong reasons. I got pregnant once by mistake and once because I allowed it to happen. I thought it was going to fix things; being pregnant has no power to fix anything. I was young, in love, and foolish. I looked around at my surroundings and thought getting pregnant too young was just normal.

Being pregnant twice in high school was once by accident and once by choice. It is hard to explain my thinking at that point in my life because I wasn't really thinking. I did not plan for making wise choices, so I made poor choices.

I was not ready to be a mother. It was selfish of me to bring her into my life and to go on trying to live my life as if my choices had no consequences. My daughter's life could have ended badly for her in continuing a family cycle of bad choices.

I was not able to give her what she needed at my level of maturity at that time. I had my mom and my dad in the house for support. My daughter did not experience that growing up because I was not with her father as she was growing up.

Something inside me said I didn't need to be here. It was a combination of fear and realization that my old life had bad outcomes built in. I left my daughter behind though. I did it for myself, and I did it for her. It could have gone very badly if I didn't finally make the decision to grow up. Looking back, it was good for me to get past these things in myself and in my life.

When I was finally ready to live up to my responsibilities, it was good that I had a support system in place. The majority of my energy then and later went to making ends meet. I did my best not to show my daughter the struggle that was a part of our lives. I did not want that to be a burden on her mind. When we faced eviction threats and disconnection notices, I shouldered that myself and hid those moments from her as best I could.

Her teenage years were a fearful time for me as a mother. There was so much that could go wrong and I knew about a lot of those things first hand. While trying to get her through those times, while still trying to make ends meet, I let my job consume me. I missed some of the more precious moments trying to avoid disaster. I remember being tired. A lot of evenings were dragging in to take care of dinner, homework, and bed. There was not much energy or time for anything else.

Over time, we adapt to a life of getting by physically, emotionally, and in every other way. We just try to get by. We do what we can to make it. What we lose in that process is the kitchen table talk. We give up that socialization with family where we recount our days and reflect together. As children get older, we disconnect from their homework and no longer interact over it. My mom didn't help me much with my homework either. She had her jobs, and my homework was mine. It was easy for me to fall into that with my own daughter with all I had to do.

We missed out on that bonding time. She took food upstairs and I didn't bother stopping her because I had my own work to do. Some nights I would drag in at nine or ten o'clock anyway. If I could do it all again differently, then I would look for ways to shut it off. I did not know how to do that. Paying the bills was on the forefront of my mind all the time as my daughter was growing up. Even knowing all that worry didn't help, it didn't change my thinking.

It took me until her senior year to realize that I was giving up more than I was gaining in that approach. Things were falling through the cracks in our relationship. She would call or text me to remind me to put together lunch money for her or to pick her up from an event. By itself, that's not a bad thing, but I began to realize that she was seeing that I was frazzled and she was constantly concerned that I would forget. She had a point. I made a point in that final year to take a step back and to take in more of my time with her. Earlier would have been better, but late beats never.

Even as she went off to college I started to discover that I still did not have balance. I had attributed everything I was sacrificing with time with what I was doing with my daughter. The truth was that my life was out of balance, my time was eaten up by that imbalance, and even with my daughter off on her own at college, my life was the same hectic pace it had always been. My life still lacked balance, and I let my myriad responsibilities take their toll.

I was working more from home, but finding that I wasn't creating a stopping point for myself to cut work off. I was still searching for that balance. I still had a void in my life that was eating up all my time and giving me nothing in return for all that sacrifice.

I'm not thinking about marriage at this point. I know that can be fulfilling when the right two people come together in the right way, but I'm not in the right place for that. That balance and selflessness need to come first before that relationship can be healthy and full. I'm still a bit selfish with my time and that phase in my life has not yet come. I haven't always been making time for family time either. I've tried to take some more time for family, but something is still missing.

I'm not complete yet. I realize that satisfaction in my life is connected to fulfilling my purpose. I can allow myself to be consumed by my job, but that is not exactly my purpose. I can be working constantly and never take time for myself. I need to take some note of myself and my life. I need to leave work at work in order to have any time to pursue my purpose and calling in life. I have to disconnect from electronics and reduce my distractions.

I've decided to set aside at least two hours of time for myself daily. This can be meditation, the gym, prayer, reflection, or any number of other fulfilling activities. If I don't claim the time, then it will be claimed for me. It's not going to get any better unless I make it better. I don't have the time otherwise. I have deadlines to meet, and I want to be able to clean my house. All of these things fall through the cracks if you have zero control over your time.

I can take on so many tasks that I'm not able to find time for what I consider important in life. I agree to do a reading for a scripture at church, but that is one more thing I have memorize. It could be important and helpful, but it could also steal time from other things that are important.

I'm getting past the time for excuses. We make time for what we consider important. We put forth the effort to claim that time when it truly, deeply matters to us. We also make choices about making time for the little things in life. I need to take time to call my mom. When I avoid talking with my mom, it reflects the pattern in my life where I want my daughter to make time to talk to me. It is history repeating itself. I could spend hours on the phone when I have other stuff to do, but I have to decide what is important.

Having a lot to do can be stressful, but not finishing things is stressful too. Creative people don't like being in a box. It can have a tendency to lead us to jump from one task to another. If we don't commit to finishing those tasks that are truly important to us, then it adds stress to our lives.

We have to make room for our gifts to be used if we expect to flourish in life. We put off chasing our dreams because we say we'll have more time in due time, but when is that? When it comes to pursuing our gifts and purpose in life, we can hear God saying to us, "Show me." It means the time to make time for what is most important and what is God's best is now. Carve out the time now. Balance is found in making that time that matches our true priorities. Don't wait to live your life. Take the time back from those things that steal time from you.

Psalm 62:8

Trust in him at all times, you people; pour out your hearts to him, for God is our refuge.

CHAPTER 26: I WANT MY FAMILY BACK

The past six months have been hard for me. The entire process of finding my purpose has been a struggle and my life during the course of writing this book has taken more twists and turns than I can count or completely remember.

Years ago, I was struggling to find the determination to go forward and to set goals. I didn't fully know it during the darkest times of my life, but I was building my testimony of finding my purpose through my struggles. The darkness and trials I'm going through now are still serving that same testimony building purpose.

My grandmother passed away. She was an important part of my life and an important part of this book. In closing out her life's testimony here in this chapter, I seek to continue to carry her and the lessons I learned from her life with me as I fulfill my purpose. As I head up women's ministries at my church or I speak at events, I'm honoring her by honoring my purpose.

I knew she was sick. My mother had downplayed it so that none of us grandchildren fully knew how sick she really was. I already don't go home as often as probably should, so it was easy to buy into the version of the story my mother was telling - and not telling.

My grandmother had fallen earlier in the year. She had been dealing with alcoholism for a while and that had come more to light recently. She had reached the point that she got the trembles and shakes when she couldn't get a drink. She had been masking it all for years. Alcohol had become her fuel and her source.

I'm sorry that she felt like she had to hide it. People looked up to her and she did not want to lose that. In her last days, she had decided just to forget all the appearances. People could see it in her. She had dark rings around her eyes.

They told us finally that she wasn't keeping food down. They started looking for cancer because of a lump they found in her throat. They discovered esophageal cancer. Alcohol abuse is connected to this form of cancer sometimes and can increase the risk of developing it.

I came home for Christmas. She was in the hospital, as she had been for a while, and the holidays were different for not having her around.

I went to see her. I almost could not recognized her. She was so thin. She had been in there too long and they couldn't let her go home in her condition anymore. They were feeding her through an IV.

I said to her, "You need to stick around for my daughter's graduation."

My grandmother said okay. I'm not sure if she believed she could make it at that point or if she was just humoring me.

I told her I was writing this book and that I wanted to dedicate it to her. She gave me her blessing for it. She wanted me to tell my truth and fulfill my purpose. That meant a lot to me.

She had told me more than once long before she was in the hospital sick. "Don't come home. Stay in D.C. There's nothing here for you that you need to worry about."

This wasn't a rejection on her part. She just did not want me to be dragged down by the world she saw around her. She did not want me to fall into trouble and out of success like she saw others doing. If I was making a life for myself, she wanted me to stick with that and pursue it instead of moving backward.

My grandmother reminded me of the character Madea. There is truth behind the attitude and energy in that character. My grandmother was like that and people were drawn to her energy and her soul behind all the other trouble she faced – maybe because of it too.

She could not whisper. Everything came out loud and clear. There was no missing what she was saying or why she was saying it.

It was so hard to see her in a state of decline and weakness. For her to be so weak and quiet to the point that is was hard to hear her was jarring to say the least. She was not a helpless woman and it was unnerving to see her reduced to a helpless state in the hospital bed. It took a toll on me.

I took a long hard look at myself. At my best, I achieve many of the great qualities I had seen in her. At my worst, I see myself going after her mistakes. I could see myself in that bed, weak and alone, if I do not make different and better choices in my life. She is my example and my warning at the same time. I saw my potential future there and I intended to change that course for my life.

I wept.

She couldn't be herself around certain members of the family. There is a tendency among some to lean toward the critical, especially if they saw weakness or shortcomings. This is not a good thing and it cost us opportunities for healing as a family. It cost us connections.

My grandmother expressed to me regrets as she looked back on her life. It was not as much her mistakes which were her more obvious regrets, but also the missed opportunities. She wished that she had built up some different things for herself and the family during her life. She wished that she had traveled. I took those lessons to heart and plan to do differently because of them. There was so much she wanted to do and the doors to those opportunities were closed to her.

I left there and went to the CVS. It was Christmas, so it was one of the only places open. I bought three or four bottles of wine. All I wanted to do was mask my pain for a while. In that moment, I was back in that place. I hadn't understood how bad her condition was and it threw me for a loop.

I called my cousin and asked if I could come over with my latest purchases. I feel like I can hang out with family that is on the outside. I've spent enough time there during my life. I spent enough time hiding like my grandmother had to do.

As I tried to drink away my problems that night at my cousin's house; we began to mix in some of the bootleg liquor that is popular in some parts of the South. I discovered the hard way that my tolerance for drinking was down and that wine and bootleg liquor don't mix well. I got sick. I got very, very sick.

After I stayed there trying to nurse off the effects of a night of cutting loose and covering up pain, I just wanted to leave. I only came home two or three times a year anyway and this trip was turning into nothing but pain. I couldn't wait to get home to DC.

As time went on, my daughter's eighteenth birthday came around. My mom wasn't able to come because my grandmother was still in the hospital.

They moved my grandmother to hospice. I was in denial about what that meant. Someone had to break it down for me and I still wasn't accepting the truth of it. I still wanted to think it was care and recovery instead of the final days with nothing else to do but to manage the pain. It had been going on for months at that point.

It was February 27th. It was a Friday. It was the day after my brother's birthday. I got a text that Granny had passed away at five that morning.

My daughter had a strong reaction to the loss. It was the first time she had really gone through a loss like that. She had only been about three or four when my aunt was shot and killed, so she does not remember that.

After she was off to college, I was left home on my own to deal with all of this.

I broke down.

I don't want to be exactly like her, but I want to be like her in some ways. I want to be blunt. I admired that in her. There was honesty and truth in that part of her. There was potential for healing and connection. I didn't want to be the person that had to be ashamed or outside our family support system. I didn't want to hide behind a mask of everything being okay.

I told my mom I wanted to say some words at the funeral. I ended up sharing some of the positives while saying that she wasn't always a saint.

We ran into family at the funeral we had not seen in a while.

When her son left, he took his family with him down to Atlanta and did not stay in contact. That was fifteen or twenty years ago. At the funeral, he had already had a drink. He was masking his own pain with a problem he had for a long time that made him separate from the rest of the family.

Talking to my cousins that were now adults was like talking to strangers. We found ourselves focusing on the thin memories from back when we were children. How did the time go by, we asked. I felt like I didn't know them.

After talking to that side of the family, I found that they felt like we were too good for them and they couldn't be themselves. They couldn't reach out to us. The children had no connection to us when they grew up, so as I told my mom, it shouldn't have been left to them. It was on us to reach out and we didn't.

As I looked through my grandmother's things, I found that she was a writer. She wrote letters as if to God about all the things she was dealing with. The writing was emotional and she did not want to be alone.

I find myself up against the wall and I don't want to be the person that has to take a drink to deal with the pain. I took a step back and realized I was starting to drink more. After work, I went from having a glass to coming closer to finishing a bottle. I discovered I could hold my liquor again.

Instead of just trying to cut back on my drinking, I decided to address the underlying problems this time. My anxiety had kicked back in. When my daughter went off to college, another void was added there in my life. The first two or three weeks had been hard.

Anxiety and depression are the most common forms of mental illness that we deal with. Life changing situations hit us and then we build up these things. I hit a point where I was scared to go to sleep at night because my chest hurt from it and I was afraid I wouldn't wake up and was too afraid to call my family as I was the one that was looked up to having it all together or least tried to portray that I did.

I'm working on changing my mindset. I've chosen not to be worried for my daughter. I gave that over to God. Worry is not faith, and I have to trust. I just pray that we can build a stronger relationship and not continue the cycle of generational upbringings.

Not a day goes by that I don't think of my Granny. I feel her watching over me. I don't want to let her down. I feel her whispering in my ear. "Baby girl, you can do this."

I want to have my family back. I want to reconnect with them in an honest and meaningful way. Time heals all wounds. Healing requires honesty. My purpose requires honesty. I finally understood that I could not change my past or people but I could change my position and my perspective on certain situations

AFTERWORD: THE NEXT CHAPTER

By reading this book, you have helped me with my purpose. You have heard my story in my voice. If this book has helped you in any way, then maybe you are on your way to meeting your purpose. Perhaps you are on your way to a new chapter in your life. There is no reason you can't change your path now.

Finishing this book was a powerful force toward changing my life. Many opportunities have opened for me because I saw this through. I think, as a matter of fact I know God honored my trust in Him and by seeing this through to the end. He felt I was ready for the next chapter in my life too.

This transformation happened for me as I was writing it and you saw my transformation in process.

This year was my year. It wasn't that everything was perfect; it was that I chose to act on my calling. Transformation and trying new things were not something that I had seen through to the end in my past. I missed out on a number of opportunities because of that. I was the one that made the resolutions at the beginning of the year and quit on every one of them. I was still struggling and still not complete.

At the beginning, I was asking, "Why me?"

God was answering, "Why not you?"

And so my opportunity for transformation began.

This transformation required me to change my mindset. It opened me to the blessings that God had for me. I had to put aside my negative mindset, my doubts, and my fears.

Now, I think it into existence. I can speak my success into reality. I think the part and it manifests in my favor. The same can happen for you too, if it hasn't already.

I see life differently now. I can be more when I push myself. Trials and roadblocks are different for me now. They are not the end of the journey, but a part of it. I face them now and go to Plan B instead of quitting.

God has a purpose and a timing for everything. Years ago, He wouldn't have blessed me like now. I wouldn't have been in a place to handle it, if He had. I'm in a different place now. The struggle has put me into the place to use the blessings finally.

I've started to trust and to share this project with others. The reactions of others have encouraged me, but more importantly, they have shown me the need for this story and discussion to be out there for others. Sometimes just hearing the title gets a reaction from a person in a place of need.

This has been a therapy for me as telling one's story often is. I hope in reading it you have found motivation, encouragement, and empowerment.

I'm praying more and differently. I have a new job and a new outlook. I'm already overcoming roadblocks and challenges in this new position. I came in and had to work to get everyone on the same page. The second week I was there, I started to feel buyer's remorse. I started to have doubts and ask why I was there at all. During the adjustment, I had to share an office and I was outside my comfort zone.

By the third week, I was looking for other work again. I was not having an impact right away and I was ready to give up again. I prayed about it.

The answer came: I find strength in my struggles. I am to finish what I've started now. My struggle this time was that I'm used to things being a certain way. In my new position, I'm not getting my way in everything. I'm being challenged and pushed.

So, I prayed, I meditated, and I lifted up my concerns.

God has timing and purpose in what we face in life. I'm here because God blessed me here. I'm being stretched. I'm being taken out of my comfort zone so that I can grow.

Be careful what you ask for. Be specific in your prayers. Once you get what you want, don't turn around and question the blessing. God expects us to transform and act once we are blessed and especially with the blessings we ask Him for.

I realized I got blessed to the point that I am able to move forward in ways I could not before. I've been able to pay off bills and put a lump sum away in savings to invest in my dreams.

I see the blessing and now I understand it. I understand where it is meant to lead me.

A good friend told me, "I see you. I knew you six years ago and I see the difference. I see something in you. You are in a place to be truly successful. I see how this change has made you passionate in seeking that success."

She said she saw a new chapter starting in my life. I can see a new chapter starting in your life, too, from taking the time to read this and consider your purpose. Please, see your struggles in life and where they are meant to lead you. Use them as the beginning of your transformation into what you were meant to be.

My purpose is to help people and I pray my story has served to help you. I am meant to use my voice and these pages are a part of that. I'm here to help, to assist, and to encourage. I'm here to inspire others.

I didn't have that before, but we are here now. Begin your transformation, find your purpose, and see your journey through as the best is yet to come. Life is too short to hold grudges, act off pettiness, focus on negativity, or just be weary and stuck.

Procrastination will keep you from your destination. Motivation will get you on track to determination that results in manifestation. Start encouraging yourself, find that "me" moment that brings satisfaction be it via prayer, meditation or just treating yourself to something rewarding like a spa day or a vacay that stimulates the mindset to know you can do anything that your heart desires. Stay focused. Stay true to yourself. The purpose that you have started has now begun.

Made in the USA
Middletown, DE
08 July 2017